Classic Diners of Vermont

ERIN K. McCORMICK

AMERICAN PALATE

Published by American Palate
A Division of The History Press
Charleston, SC
www.historypress.com

All images are from the author's collection unless otherwise noted.

First published 2018

Manufactured in the United States

ISBN 9781467140126

Library of Congress Control Number: 2018945795

Notice: The information in this book is true and complete to the best of our knowledge. It is offered without guarantee on the part of the author or The History Press. The author and The History Press disclaim all liability in connection with the use of this book.

Classic Diners of Vermont

ERIN K. McCORMICK

For all Vermonters—near and far, by birth or by choice—
who come together to build communities and break down walls.

For Nanny, my ninety-six-year-old grandmother, who introduced me to the diner at an early age, instilled in me an appreciation for simple pleasures and embodies the warmth and community spirit classic diners exude.

For Nick, who is endlessly supportive of new Vermont adventures and is the best road trip companion a girl could ask for.

CONTENTS

INTRODUCTION

Crystal Diner, Lawrence Township, New Jersey.
Oversized leather booths, shiny counter stools attached at their base and coin-operated jukeboxes at every table crooning Johnny Cash, the Beatles or Elvis Presley. Waitresses flinging coffee (without a spill) and spreading genuine smiles in a seemingly effortless, ballet-like dance across the roadside eatery—always doting, never rushed. Crispy pork roll and shit on a shingle (or Taylor Ham and chipped beef, if you prefer), perfectly paired with eggs—over medium—and toasted homemade rye bread with just the right amount of melted butter and fruit jam from the little packets sitting out on the table. Now known as the Route 1 Diner, Crystal was the diner of my youth—that is, the American diner that made an imprint on me in my formative years. We all have one…don't we? A diner where we shared meals as a family… An eatery where we told stories, recounted our days and reconnected as a family and with community members…A source of hearty home cooking at affordable prices in a come-as-you-are casual setting…A vanishing, vintage piece of Americana and an emblem of simpler times.

LEARNING TO LOVE VERMONT

When I moved to Middlebury, Vermont, in 2004 to attend Middlebury College in the west-central part of the state, I never once looked back to my roots in New Jersey—even for an egg, cheese and pork roll sandwich on a sesame bagel, however tempting. Once in Vermont, I began noticing the phrase "Don't Jersey Vermont" on bumper stickers, typically on Subaru Outbacks and Honda Elements around the state—the unofficial cars of Vermont, I soon learned. I immediately understood the stereotypical sticker. It was clear to me just how different the Vermont lifestyle is from how and where I grew up.

The sense of place and pride Vermonters feel for where they live is unique and special. The Vermont brand is wholly different from that brand in New Jersey I grew up with. In Vermont, there are few major highways, no high-rises and no billboards to crowd the landscape. In fact, billboards are illegal and have been since 1968, when the Green Mountain State passed an anti-billboard law to protect the roadsides from advertising campaigns, which would, in essence, disrupt the untouched nature of Vermont's natural beauty. Traffic is infrequent outside the cities. When there is traffic, it's most often caused by an agricultural vehicle hogging up two lanes, an escaped cow or other farm animal on the run or neighbors stopping to chat quickly with someone they know, not paying attention to who or what might be coming up behind them. Vermonters are patient. They will wave and go around, never (or rather infrequently) using their car horns to cause a stir or a scene. Vermonters joke that the only time they lock their vehicles is during harvest season—that is, late summer, when zucchini are plentiful. Locals joke that if you're not careful, you'll wind up being "gifted" zucchini in the back seat of your car. This gesture epitomizes what it means to be a Vermonter: Vermonters are resourceful and caring with a playful sense of humor.

Safety and serenity are huge draws for many to Vermont, whether visiting or making Vermont home, especially for the back-to-your-roots, simple lifestyle and rich quality of life the Green Mountain State affords. The Vermont brand is rooted in the land and the outdoors, the beauty of the place we are lucky to call home. The Vermont brand is defined by our industries—milk, maple syrup, skiing and, now, craft beer. Above all else though, the Vermont brand is centered on community. This notion is underscored, reinforced and reflected in the classic diners of Vermont that are epicenters of community and play a vital role in the lives of the locals they serve.

During my time in college, I used weekends to explore winding mountain roads with long vistas at the peak; to visit hole-in-the-wall general stores with penny candy, antiques and real operating mailrooms; and to explore independent eateries—whether family restaurants, sandwich shops, bakeries, brewpubs or fine-dining establishments—that play a role in bringing together Vermonters and visitors alike. I began getting to know the geography and history of Vermont better than even New Jersey, my home state for eighteen years. I took an interest in the 251 Club, an organization of Vermont enthusiasts who have a shared goal of visiting the 251 towns and cities in Vermont. By visiting, I don't mean just driving through those towns either. Every visit to a town or city in Vermont is purposeful. Each of the 251 towns and cities in Vermont is worthy of a becoming a destination in order to experience the location and the real and genuine people who call it home.

In my travels to diners throughout Vermont as I began researching for this book, I was continually overwhelmed to see how many diners remain the hearts and souls of their communities, wherever they may be in Vermont. The location doesn't matter. The specific community doesn't matter. Even the diner's length of time in its community doesn't matter *that* much. There are new diners in Vermont that aren't classic in style or rich in history that still bring people together. They still serve the purpose for which diners were first established. Diners are where locals come together for conversations with their neighbors and for small talk with strangers. Diners are where people know they'll be accepted and welcomed no matter what they look like, what they're wearing or where they're from. Diners are where those who might not have anyone at home come for companionship and a warm smile across the countertop, a bottomless cup of coffee or a big slice of homemade pie. Diners are an extension of home.

During a time when technology reigns supreme, diners are a chance to take a step back, slow down and truly be together. Diners embody what Vermont is at its core—a place where everyone is welcomed, where we get to know our neighbors and where we celebrate our togetherness rather than dwell on our differences. Despite all odds, diners remain vital gathering places and are continuing to grow in popularity, with a resurgence in vintage diners and drive-ins across America. Through social media platforms like Facebook and Instagram, young diner-goers are capturing and preserving the evolution of the diner in its current form. Copious iPhone photos of hearty breakfasts, vintage mugs, stunning stained-glass details, polished chrome, intricate and colorful tile work and oversized milkshakes capture the essence of today's diner. Young generations are taking to social media to showcase the togetherness they experience in diners around Vermont, over coffee, corned beef hash and conversation.

My hope is that this book too, like the current preservation and promotion of diner culture through social media, will capture the history, showcase the evolution of the diner car and tell the stories of Vermont's classic diners.

The next time you see a classic roadside diner, stop in—no matter where you are. Take an hour out of your hurried day to pull over. Enjoy a meal in celebration of what has come before you and how times have changed. You owe it to yourself and to whomever you're with to be in the moment. Belly up to the counter or slide into a booth. Engage in conversation without thinking of where you need to be or what you need to do. Listen to what someone else has to say. Smile at someone you don't know. Enjoy the sights, sounds and smells of home. Welcome to Vermont.

Chapter 1

MADE IN VERMONT

In order to appreciate what makes Vermont's classic diners so special, one must truly understand the essence of Vermont. Vermont has so many defining characteristics that make it unique and define not only the small state itself but also its people. Vermont and Vermonters are rooted in and proud of the Green Mountain State's brand. After all, the people have helped create it and shape it. To outsiders who might have little to no direct experience with Vermont, the Vermont brand still means something. Vermont may be the sixth-smallest state by size and the second-smallest by population in the United States, but the Vermont brand is well known, well respected and well received by locals and travelers alike, arguably the most of any of the fifty states.

At its core, the Vermont brand is idyllic with an unspoiled landscape. Vermont is uncrowded and unhurried, largely void of traffic, billboards and high-rise buildings. Vermont is the land of historic covered bridges, red barns popping out from a lush landscape and worn, rusty metal silos with a backdrop of snow-covered ski trails. Vermont is taking in a sunset over the mountains. Vermont is sitting in a well-loved Adirondack chair by a fire pit, enjoying the smell of hardwood mixed with ample fresh air. Vermont is outdoor adventure: canoeing on Lake Bomoseen, hiking Camel's Hump or skiing down Sterling at Smugglers' Notch. Vermont's brand is worn, red-checkered flannel shirts and woolen blankets. Vermont is frozen nostrils, fresh tracks at daylight and craft beer for après-ski. Vermont is down-home cooking that's rooted in healthy, local ingredients that are grown and raised in our backyards. Vermont is long summer nights spent stargazing and chasing fireflies or swims in swimming holes, dips in streams and boating in lakes. Vermont and the quality of life it affords is pure, simple and serene.

Food is at the core of the Vermont lifestyle. With the working landscape in Vermont, so much of the culture and brand is rooted in growing and producing. Apple orchards contribute to the extensive hard cider business now prevalent in Vermont. Hop farms are producing bittering agents for the craft beer scene. Numerous dairy farms throughout the state are producing milk, of course, but also contributing to the plethora of locally made cheese—winning awards for quality and innovation around the globe. Vermont is rooted in the buy-local, shop-small philosophy. With so many producers in the state, supporting your neighbor is what Vermonters do. With this arguably comes a certain cache or organic attraction about something that's "made in Vermont." When people think of Vermont, they think first of maple syrup—the refined, nearly see-through Grade A or the rustic, earthy-tasting Grade B. And pancakes, of course. They think of that Vermont liquid gold on pancakes and waffles. They think of cheese and milk—of Cabot Cheese. They think of grass-fed meats, golden yolk eggs and fresh produce sourced from the farm down the road.

In 2006, the State of Vermont passed Rule CF 120 Representation of Vermont Origin Rule to regulate usage of the word "Vermont" on products and packaging. To be a Vermont product, a significant portion of the product must be made in Vermont and be of a Vermont origin. Because the Vermont brand carries so much weight, this rule was put into effect to guarantee that products or services carrying the Vermont name are indeed tied to Vermont. The purpose of the rule is to prevent consumers from being misled, while also protecting and rewarding authentic Vermont businesses that are contributing to the local economy and creating jobs throughout the state. With so much goodness coming out of Vermont, this rule preserves the value of the brand and protects those who live, breathe and help build the brand daily through Vermont's own products.

Although diners are typically known for inexpensive home cooking, many of Vermont's diners are incorporating local products from nearby farms and proudly celebrating their relationships with neighborhood producers. Quite a few diners in Vermont are now showcasing these local partnerships, becoming even more attached to the Vermont brand. An authentic diner announcement—made of movable white letters on a black background situated over the counter at the Parkway Diner in South Burlington—celebrates local products from Shadow Cross Farms in Colchester, Cabot Creamery in Cabot, Branon's West View Maples from Fairfield and Pomykala Farm in Grand Isle. At the Country Girl Diner in Chester, local maple syrup from Mitch's Maple Syrup is for sale. Located "right here in Chester," the sign announces pints, quarts and half gallons for sale on-site, accompanied by a fun fact that forty gallons of sap are needed to create just one gallon of syrup.

And you won't find mass-produced maple syrup at Vermont diners; authentic maple syrup is a must and an expectation. In fact, maple syrup is a significant flavor in sweet treats at diners throughout the state. At the Country Girl Diner, Maple Walnut Pie is a staple for dessert. At the Miss Lyndonville Diner in the Northeast Kingdom, Maple Cream Pie is a draw. At many diners, like Henry's Diner in Burlington and Bob's Diner in Manchester Center, Vermont Maple Milkshakes round out the maple offerings, or you can try a Maple Mocha Shake from the Birdseye Diner in Castleton. At the Birdseye Diner, not only is a thirty-two-ounce jug of local maple syrup offered for sale, but it's offered with pancake mix and blueberry pancake mix from the Brown Family Farm, a local sugaring operation in the diner's community.

With the rise in the popularity of craft beer in Vermont, some diners across the state are also starting to offer draught pours for their diner-goers, tying into one of the largest tourism industries in the state. Vermont has more breweries per capita than any other state in the nation. More micro-breweries and nano-breweries pop up every year. In fact, craft beer has surpassed the maple syrup industry and ski industry in terms of income produced through tourism in Vermont. The beer industry also creates a significant number of jobs for workers in the state. It's not uncommon at diners to find local beers on tap. At Chelsea Royal Diner in Brattleboro, favorites like Fiddlehead IPA and Switchback Brewing Company's unfiltered ale round out the beverage offerings, which also include milkshakes and bottomless coffee. At Bob's Diner in Manchester Center, it's not an uncommon sight to see folks enjoying a flight of beer with lunch after a morning of outlet shopping, adventuring outdoors or skiing at Stratton Mountain.

So much of Vermont is reflected in diners throughout the state. Like many other places, Vermont's diners are rooted in community and serve people of all walks of life. When you walk through any diner in Vermont, you will be treated as family. You will enjoy home-cooked, made-from-scratch meals in laidback, casual settings. In Vermont's diners, you will be taken back to simpler times, rooted in conversation and getting to know your neighbors. Perhaps most importantly, in Vermont's diners, you can come to understand what makes Vermont so special—the essence of Vermont, the Vermont brand.

DEFINING COUNTER CULTURE AT VERMONT'S CLASSIC DINERS

Not dissimilar from other states in New England or the Tri-State area with a significant presence of classic diners, the counter culture in Vermont remains strong and withstands the evolution of time. With how much changes regularly in our lives, from new technologies and innovations to politics and environmental change to shifts in the economy, the changes in the world of the classic diner are much less significant. Change in general is minimized, even mitigated. Life goes on, but in diners, everything remains the same. In fact, diner owners go to great lengths to ensure their diners don't change over time. They fight the inevitable passage of time. They stay rooted in the simplicity of the past that has become a draw in and of itself.

The beauty and appeal of the diner is that it largely remains trapped in time, unlike so much else in life. Prices might increase slightly. Daily specials will shift from a hearty brisket sandwich to a fry fish of haddock and scallops. Pie flavors will change daily from apple, cherry and custard to peach, banana cream and pumpkin. Some staff might eventually leave, but the bulk of servers remain, feeling immense loyalty to their customers. On the outside, life continues to evolve. But inside a diner where the essence of the past is captured, everything stops. Everything stands still. Even the structures of classic diners manufactured by the Worcester Lunch Car Company and Silk City Diners themselves are withstanding time. Formica countertops are worn down by elbows and plates. Counter stools, sat on by generations over decades, might not swivel quite as easily as they once did. Wooden booths become squeaky, the home to many laughs and candid conversation over the years. Original coolers still keep creamers cold. Chrome and stainless-steel accents remain shiny, almost reflective. Neon signs still illuminate the surroundings and are a welcome sign of life inside, as well as the promise of hot coffee and a filling meal.

Diners are dependable places to stop when you're traveling, as you always know what to expect. At a diner, you can always be yourself. There's no need to dress a part or act like someone you're not. At diners, you are accepted as you come. You can enjoy a satisfying, warming meal while talking to someone next to you or seated in a booth behind you. Due to the size of the interior of diners, there isn't room for privacy or even much personal space. This is part of the design and the appeal of the classic diner over the years—to bring people together.

So how is counter culture defined, and how does it tie into the Vermont brand? Counter culture is sassy waitresses who are sharp-witted and quick to serve a hot cup of coffee with the spoon already in the cup. Counter culture is chatting about anything with anyone—drumming up a conversation with a stranger seated next to you. Counter culture is filling meals at friendly prices. One of the defining attributes of counter culture is the relationships formed in diners, particular the relationships between patrons that continue to deepen over time. Once just familiar faces, cooks and waitresses in diners become family to regulars at diners. They move beyond being on a first-name basis and knowing their order by memory to the point of being an extension of their family. They know where they work, what their hobbies are, who their children are. They celebrate significant life events—engagements, marriages, new additions—and feel the heartache associated with losing members of their extended diner family when the time comes.

At Vermont's diners, diner owners strive to preserve this counter culture over time. As technology continues to develop and often hinders face-to-face human relationships, diners are the common ground between all people—where conversation is the draw. Many of the classic diners in Vermont don't have a social media presence or a website. They don't need to advertise. They are community institutions that are rooted in word-of-mouth endorsement and the roles they play in generations of locals. Vermont's diner owners say that not much will ever change in their diners—at least they hope not. Diners are so rooted in what was, and therefore, so little ever changes. Conversations will still happen over coffee. Fluffy chocolate chip pancakes as large as the plate they're served on will still be scarfed down. Diner owners will still claim their homemade corned beef hash is the best in the state (perhaps you'll just have to taste them all yourself to decide for certain). Regulars will still visit one time, or maybe three times, a day for coffee, a slice of pie and just to say hi. Some say you can't go back, but in Vermont, you always can to celebrate the past while living in the present at the classic diners across the state.

THE SOUL OF VERMONT COMMUNITIES

Diners are often at the center of the communities in which they reside, both literally and figuratively. They are an icon of American culture and provide a quintessential American experience. When you step into a diner, you know what to expect, no matter the location. Diners never change. They withstand time and technology, embodying the essence of what came before us…of what used to be. What makes a diner special is what the diner provides, of course, but also what the patrons contribute to the culture of the diner. There's a distinct, friendly energy that diners exude. As the owner of the Country Girl Diner in Chester, Jessica Holmes, said, "The diner is the soul of our community." With most diners being open every day and at least for breakfast and lunch hours, with a handful in Vermont serving dinner as well, they are always welcoming and ready for the next patron to enter the door. They're not corporate, polished (other than the stainless steel and chrome) or pretentious. Patrons become like family. Regulars are always known on a first-name basis, and at some diners in Vermont, regulars even have a special button in the computer for a particular customer's everyday meal—that is, if the diner has even progressed to automated ordering. Holmes said that at the Country Girl Diner, they probably have thirty patrons who come in daily for either breakfast or lunch or sometimes both.

Many of Vermont's diners are located in college towns, helping to bridge generations and unify communities, including:

The Birdseye in Castleton, home to Castleton University
Henry's Diner in downtown Burlington, home of the University of Vermont
The Parkway Diner in South Burlington, near St. Michael's College and Champlain College
The Blue Benn in Bennington, home to Bennington College
Miss Lyndonville Diner in Lyndonville, home to Lyndonville State College
Tot's Diner in Poultney, home to Green Mountain College
The Diner in Middlebury, home to Middlebury College

College students work in these diners. They also frequent the local eateries that have become destinations in their college towns as a chance to escape cafeteria meals, get off campus and load up on hearty portions at fair prices. Diners are known for people watching and striking up conversations with strangers. In these towns, it's common to see college students chatting with generations of regulars—many of whom have been visiting daily for

This advertisement for the Country Girl Diner features Dolly, an owner of the diner in the 1960s. *Courtesy of Jessica Holmes.*

years. The diner, after all, is now more than ever an institution that brings millennials and baby boomers together in the essence of what diners have always been and have so organically have achieved. In Vermont's diners, it's a mixture of young and old, of new and seasoned diner-goers. Sit at the worn lunch counter in a Vermont diner. Watch and wait. Take a look around you, and you'll quickly see how the young and old come together. It's a beautiful thing to see generations bonding over a shared passion. College students ask regulars questions about how life used to be "back then." Regulars share a glimpse of the simple life they used to live, still embodied in the diner they frequent. After all, diners at their core are a place to share and learn from one another. Diners foster common ground between generations. Today, diners act as a unifier among disparate people with a shared affinity for good grub and conversation over coffee or perhaps a maple milkshake.

A Family Affair at Vermont's Classic Diners

In Vermont, some diners, like the Springfield Royal Diner in Springfield, have undergone rather frequent ownership changes due to the challenges with running a small-scale restaurant business. Others, like Miss Lyndonville, the Blue Benn and the Oasis Diner before its closing, have been largely operated by the same family, spanning generations. Even today, many of the operations of diners remain in the family. For the Country Girl Diner,

Holmes and her husband, Paul, own and operate the business, and Paul cooks with his son Zack 90 percent of the time. Their eleven-year-old daughter comes in to bake with Holmes as well, contributing to the family-oriented nature of the establishment.

The Blue Benn in Bennington has been run by husband-and-wife team Sonny and Marylou Monroe, now with help from daughter Lisa Monroe LaFlamme as well. The Windsor Diner in Windsor started off as an endeavor between father Fred Borcuk and his daughter Theresa Taylor. Libby's Blue Line Diner, now the Athens Diner in Colchester, was started by a mother-and-daughter pair. Husband-and-wife team Todd Darrah and Janet Picard have owned and operated the Chelsea Royal Diner together since 1990. Husband-and-wife team Bill and Naomi Maglaris purchased Henry's Diner in Burlington and later the Athens Diner in Colchester. Naomi said, "I have poured my heart into Henry's to make my husband's dream come true," speaking to the partnership and dedication to preserving and promoting the classic diner many diner families in Vermont have. More often than not, operating the classic Vermont diner is a family affair. This is especially true for the diners in Vermont that have become staples in their communities and true destinations for travelers and locals. The classic Vermont diner has become the center of a family and of the community it serves.

Chapter 2
CLASSIC DINERS OF VERMONT

A BRIEF HISTORY OF THE AMERICAN DINER

American diners were born in the mid- to late nineteenth century, at which time they were mobile. They traveled from one place to another, similar to the modern-day food truck. Walter Scott, a pressman and entrepreneur in Providence, Rhode Island, is credited with coming up with the concept for the American diner. Scott began preparing food—largely sandwiches, egg dishes and coffee—part time in 1873 in a modified horse-pulled freight wagon in the evenings. His goal was to service late-night workers and pressmen who couldn't find open eateries elsewhere. Once his business began to take off, he gave up his press position to operate his evening lunch wagon full time. No matter the time of day, inexpensive, accessible food was a model that was proving itself to be quite lucrative. Other businessmen took note. They, too, began converting horse-drawn wagons, streetcars and trolleys into rolling restaurants that offered walk-up service, along with room for a few guests to sit down and enjoy a meal inside at a counter. These early lunch cars had basic stoves and iceboxes and a few interior seats. They were largely devoid of anything homey. In fact, these establishments ended up being banned in some locations such as Buffalo and Atlantic City for the bad manners of the patrons, coupled with the often beat-up and battered appearances of many lunch wagons. Maintenance and upkeep of the mobile, roadside eateries was often lacking.

Starting at dawn, the Parkway Diner is ready to serve its regulars.

At that time, many lunch wagons were traveling to workplaces and jobsites to serve hungry workers over lunch and in the evening hours as well. Lunch wagons became known as places for a square meal, big slice of pie and hot cup of coffee at an affordable price. These nineteenth-century diners provided a service that brought workers together for cheap, quick meals and offered a pause in their workday. Eventually, with the popularity of lunch wagons taking off, towns and cities began adding restrictions to the number of wagons in certain areas, along with their times of operation. Serving a real need for the patrons they fed, however, the owners of the wagons were forced to find more permanent locations, which eventually made the case for prefabricated dining establishments and the evolution of the lunch wagon into the dining car. The largely stationary dining car units were assembled off-site and trucked to more permanent locations for installation.

By the 1900s, there were largely three companies manufacturing lunch cars. Tierney Dining Cars, Worcester Lunch Car Company and Jerry O'Mahony Diners were leading the diner industry in manufacturing. As time went on, the wheels on the structures got smaller and smaller. The premanufactured structures became more permanent in their locations. The first stationary lunch car came from the Jerry O'Mahony Diner Company in 1913. Around that time, manufacturers began to install larger counters, include intricate tile work in the design and even add bathrooms to offer more services to their patrons.

During and after World War I, lunch car owners began to realize that they needed more patrons to remain profitable and stay in business. Up until the 1920s, lunch cars were largely providing a service to male workers. They had a reputation as greasy spoons, appealing to a largely male clientele. With women's right to vote also came a shift in focus to attracting women patrons to lunch cars. Dining car owners started better maintaining and cleaning the semipermanent roadside eateries to make them more appealing to women. Business owners began adding booths and tables in addition to the already present counter stools. They painted their cars, and some even wallpapered the interiors. They added flower boxes and landscaping. They begin to advertise their fare as "home-cooked meals" to appeal to more women. Around that time, many diners took on a "Miss" in their names to soften the diner's appeal and attract more female patrons. In Vermont, despite numerous name changes over the years, the Miss Lyndonville Diner in Lyndonville and Miss Bellows Falls in Bellows Falls are two examples of diners taking on the "Miss" to provide a more feminine appeal.

Not until around the late 1920s did lunch cars start to become known as diners due to their evolving design that reflected the style of the railroad dining cars of the era. And that's really when the American diner was born, with more round exteriors, chrome and stainless-steel interiors and a futuristic look and feel that was modern and inviting. The progression in the naming of diners evolved from night lunch wagon, to lunch wagon, to lunch car, then dining car and finally shortened to diner, the lingo we utilize today when referencing classic roadside eateries. Diners continued gaining in popularity, with a wide range of manufacturers producing the prefabricated buildings, including DeRaffele Manufacturing Company, Fodero Dining Car Company, Kullman Dining Car Company, Mountain View Diners Company, Silk City Diners and the original three: Tierney Dining Cars, Jerry O'Mahony Diner Company and Worcester Lunch Car Company. Formica countertops, leather booths, stainless-steel fixtures, terrazzo floors and extensive tile work began to make an appearance as dining cars became full-blown family restaurants. Unique pops of color—teals and yellows, pinks and reds—began defining the spaces, which were now drawing in male and female patrons and increasing profitability and popularity in the process.

Diners survived and even thrived during the Great Depression and World War II, largely due to the cost-effective nature of their offerings. Popularity of the diner soared into the 1950s, when diners started making their way from cities into the suburbs, following the move toward the suburban lifestyle. At this point, the iconic drive-in began to expand as well. More fast-food restaurants like McDonald's were hitting the market. By the 1960s, business at diners had begun to slip. Many classic American diners ran into financial hardship. Diners were struggling to keep up with serving home-cooked, from-scratch meals at prices in line with fast-food establishments. Life also began to speed up. Cars were faster. More people had access to them. All of a sudden, meals were being consumed on the go. People were eating in the front seats of their cars rather than at the counter inside a diner. Convenience suddenly overshadowed quality. The diner began to lose some of its relevancy as a destination for a quick and substantial meal at a fair price. Subsequently, around the 1970s, the aesthetic for diners changed from the colorful, stainless-steel clad structures with neon signs to more Mediterranean or Neoclassical-inspired, with stonework or brickwork on the façade and darker, more subdued colors. In Vermont, this change is evident in Henry's Diner in Burlington, which underwent a significant renovation to its façade in this distinct Mediterranean look and feel. This change, in essence, was to disguise diners and make them look more like family restaurants. Diners during this time reverted to their former reputation of grungy greasy spoons. Many closed their doors. Many fought to operate in the face of more competition, higher food costs and the presence of more affordable and even quicker eateries.

In the 1990s, the American affinity for classic diners was largely rekindled. It still remains strong today, largely due to the baby boomer generation. Blue plate specials and cost-effective comfort food are the draw for older and younger patrons alike. The appeal of diners now spans

As seen from across the street, here is Henry's diner when the Spanish-style building was added in front. *Courtesy of Naomi Maglaris and John Couture.*

generations. Diners attract older folks who have been frequenting diners for years, as well as the younger crowd, who appreciate the cheap, home-cooked meals, large portions and throwback vibe. Part of the resurgence in the popularity of diners is due to the media. Movies and television shows (*Happy Days* and *Saved by the Bell*, for example) depict diners as gathering places where important conversations take place and memories are made. These shows instill in a wide variety of generations the cultural importance of diners as community space. The Food Network's popular show *Diners, Drive-Ins and Dives* has also contributed to the newfound appeal of classic roadside eateries. Guy Fieri tells the stories of the diners and diner owners and showcases dishes that are unique and draw in a wide range of patrons and generations.

Coupled with a general movement away from the impersonal and unhealthy focus on fast food, along with support for the shop-local mentality, diners are once again thriving as popular eateries, especially in Vermont. Now, it's common to see a line out the door at Vermont diners in college towns, with students and the diners' regulars waiting to get inside for a wholesome, inexpensive meal to start the day. Many diners in Vermont, such as the Blue Benn in Bennington and the Parkway Diner in South Burlington, haven't expanded their seating capacity at all. This has been a conscious choice to keep the production manageable and the atmosphere personal. The unique characteristics of diners and the sometimes traditional, sometimes more innovative diner meals are now extensively captured on social media. Photos are snapped of friends and family members returning to a favorite local diner for shared meals and memories. The extensive representation of diners on social media showcases the longevity and broad appeal of these unique eateries, while also helping to tell the story of what diners mean to generations over time.

CLASSIC VERMONT DINERS BY MANUFACTURER

Because many classic diners were manufactured in New Jersey, Massachusetts and New York, as outlined above, many of them remain predominantly in the Northeast and Midwest today. New Jersey boasts the most, with six hundred diners, but for the size and population of Vermont, the historical diners throughout the state are quite widespread. The remaining classic diners in operation in Vermont are largely Silk City diners, Worcester Lunch Car

Company diners and a rare Mahony diner and Sterling diner. Some diners around the country have even made it into the National Register of Historic Places, including the Miss Bellows Falls in Bellows Falls. Before diving into the essence of each specific diner in Vermont—the defining characteristics on the interior and exterior, the ambiance and the cuisine—it's valuable to understand their origins by their distinct manufacturers.

Worcester Lunch Car Company

Worcester Lunch Car Company, started by Philip H. Duprey, who was a real estate agent at the time, was a leading manufacturer during the first half of the twentieth century. It had the reputation of quality craftsmanship. The Worchester Lunch Car Company built more than six hundred diners, traditionally with porcelain exteriors and hardwood interiors, complete with Gothic lettering on the front displaying the name of the diner, along with colorful awnings. It was based in Worcester, Massachusetts, from 1906 to 1957 and shipped largely all over the Northeast. In 1961, any remaining Worcester Lunch Car Company cars went to auction, and the company ceased operations. In Vermont, the following diners were manufactured by Worcester Lunch Car Company:

Chelsea Royal Diner, West Brattleboro: Worcester #736 from 1938
The Public House, previously the Farmers Diner, Quechee: Worcester #787 from 1946
Miss Bellows Falls, Bellows Falls: Worcester #771 from 1941, formerly Frankie and Johnnie's Diner
Parkway Diner, South Burlington: Worcester #839 from 1953, formerly Arcadia Diner
Windsor Diner, Windsor: Worcester #835 from 1952
Athens Diner, Colchester: Worcester #838 from 1953

Jerry O'Mahony Diner Company

The Jerry O'Mahony Diner Company in Elizabeth, New Jersey, produced roughly two thousand diners from 1917 to 1941 and was one of the largest diner manufacturers. Mahony Diners, Inc., an offshoot of the company, produced for only two years, from 1956 to 1958, and built four diners. Vermont is home to what is thought to be the only remaining Mahony diner still in existence, in Springfield.

Henry's Diner, Burlington: O'Mahony from 1925
Springfield Royal Diner, Springfield: Mahony from 1957

Silk City Diners

Silk City Diners were built in Paterson, New Jersey, by Paterson Wagon Company originally and then Paterson Vehicle Company from 1926 to 1964. Originally, the company produced solely wagons and then expanded its manufacturing style. At the time, Paterson was rooted in the silk manufacturing industry and thus obtained the moniker the Silk City, from which the Silk City Diner name was born. Silk City Diners, which were built six or eight at a time, were composed of a combination of stainless steel and porcelain. The diners came in a variety of color options and typically had the name of the diner horizontally displayed on the front. These diners were some of the most affordable premanufactured dining cars, which led to more production and many still being in existence. A total of 1,500 Silk City Diners were constructed, and each Silk City Diner carries a four-number tag for the year it was constructed and the order in which it was built. Some tags are even five digits for the years in which more than 100 diners were built. In Vermont, the following diners were manufactured by Silk City Diners and still remain in good shape today:

Blue Benn, Bennington: Silk City 4815 from 1948
Birdseye Diner, Castleton: Silk City from 1946, formerly Jim's Diner
Country Girl Diner, Chester: Silk City

Sterling Diners

Sterling Diners, created by the J.B. Judkins Company, were manufactured from 1936 to 1942. Sterling's Streamliner gained fame for its Art Deco appearance and two ends shaped like bullets. Although there is likely an abandoned Sterling diner in Vermont, the only operating Sterling diner is the Miss Lyndonville Diner in Lyndonville, which has been largely built over and doesn't reflect the typical style from the exterior.

Miss Lyndonville, Lyndonville: Sterling from 1939

Fodero Dining Car Company

Fodero Dining Car Company operated out of Newark and Bloomfield, New Jersey, from 1933 to 1981. Fodero diners are most often recognized for their Art Deco appearance and stainless-steel exteriors, along with their winged clocks. Fodero was known as the National Dining Car Company after 1939.

Martha's Diner, Coventry: Fodero from 1953, formerly the Monarch Diner

Mountain View Diner Company

Mountain View Diner Company was established in Singac, New Jersey, in 1938 with the goal of manufacturing prefabricated diners that were "designed to last a lifetime." These diners had rounded corners that squared off at the bottom, known as the "cowcatcher." This detail was one of the defining characteristics of its unique design. Through extensive marketing campaigns, Mountain View Diner Company ended up selling its diners with more widespread distribution across the United States. In 1956, the company stopped manufacturing of new diners, with roughly four hundred produced, after an attempt to go public failed.

Oasis Diner, Burlington: Mountain View #369 from 1954, now El Cortijo*

*The Oasis Diner is a dearly departed diner in Vermont that now operates as El Cortijo Taqueria y Cantina. The Oasis Diner was operated for more than forty years by Stratton "Stratty" Lines and was under the same ownership from 1954 to 2007. It was a popular destination for politicians, who were

known to announce their candidacy in the downtown Burlington location. President Clinton even visited the Oasis in 1996. As in many classic Vermont diners, the owner, Stratty, was the draw of the diner. He was the entertainer and unifier of all people from all walks of life. He had a strong sense of everything that was going on in town, from politics and sports to community events and town gossip. He heard it all from the patrons who daily walked through his downtown eatery's door. The diner closed in 2007, at which point it became home to a New York–style deli, Sadie Katz, and it now operates as El Cortijo. Even today, the Mexican restaurant in the same space has kept many of the elements of the diner intact, including the booths, ceiling and countertop seating, to preserve as much of the diner's character and charm as possible. You can still visit its Bank Street location and admire the unique character, embellished with some local Vermont elements, such as light fixtures from Burlington's own Conant Metal and Light.

DEFINING A CLASSIC DINER IN VERMONT

Vermonters and visitors are extremely passionate about their favorite diners throughout the state. Any eatery that brings people together and has down-home cooking can be considered a diner, no matter the ambiance or the structure of the building. Family restaurants, like Rosie's Restaurant in Middlebury or the Wayside Restaurant & Bakery in Montpelier, are strong examples of this—restaurants where the food is simple and unpretentious. The waitstaff is warm and welcoming. A diner in Vermont is more than its history and the structure in which it's built. What makes a diner a diner is the way it makes you feel and the role it plays as the heart of the community it serves.

Simply to limit the scope of this book, which is rooted in telling the story of the evolution of diners over time in Vermont, classic diners are defined as 1) diners with longevity in the communities where they are located and 2) diners that have a classic dining structure, most commonly in Vermont a Worcester Lunch Car Company dining car or Silk City dining car. The diners represented in this book are traditional in style. They are constructed primarily of metal—stainless steel, chrome and tin—and feature Formica countertops, terrazzo tiles and original griddles, cooktops and coolers. They resemble railroad cars and trolleys, although these diners were never used as such. They are stand-alone structures that are one story in height and are elongated with a long row of counter stools and booths lining the windows. There are exceptions to the rules, however, and many of these diner institutions have evolved over time and might not fit the exact look of a classic diner. Take the Diner in Middlebury, for instance. The building in its location on Merchants Row may not look the part now, but its rich history and the role it played in the community of Middlebury until recently warrants its inclusion. There are other roadside eateries, like the P&H Truck Stop in Wells River or the Fairlee Diner in Fairlee, that have been drawing in regulars, locals and travelers for many years. They encompass the Americana, retro vibe of many classic diners and have a prominent role in their local communities.

There are numerous other "diners," used loosely, in Vermont that could have been included for those looking for the coffee and conversation, large portions of feel-good home cooking and warm feeling they emit. All of these diners, even if they are not fundamentally classic in their roots, deserve celebration and recognition. They play a pivotal role in the lives of the patrons they serve and in the communities where they've grown up alongside their diner-goers over time. After all, a diner is more than the structure in which it operates. A diner is a destination. A diner is a feeling. A diner is family.

Other Diners in Vermont Worthy of a Visit

Anthony's Diner, St. Johnsbury
Dot's Restaurant, Wilmington
Erica's American Diner, Fairfax
The Guilty Plate Diner, Colchester
Halfway House Restaurant, Shoreham
Hartland Diner, Hartland
Laura B's, Milton
Maple City Diner, St. Albans
The Maple Diner, Bridgewater Commons
Martha's Diner, Coventry
Maxi's Restaurant, Waterbury
The Milton Diner, Milton
P&H Truck Stop, Wells River
Papa Pete's, Woodford
The Public House at Quechee Gorge, Quechee
Rosie's Restaurant, Middlebury
St. Albans Diner, St. Albans
The Sugar and Spice Vermont Sugar House, Mendon
Sunny Side Diner, Bennington
Tot's Diner, Poultney
The Townshend Dam Diner, Townshend
The Wayside Restaurant & Bakery, Montpelier

Chapter 3

THE ANATOMY OF A CLASSIC DINER

Classic diners are rooted in simple home cooking and classic American cuisine—homey dishes that are representative of what Grandma made in a casual, inviting and unpretentious space. In defining what constitutes a classic diner, so much of it comes down to the structure and the architecture itself, along with the warmth of the waitstaff and the price for and portions of the food. Vermont is lucky to be home to a number of traditional dining cars that are still in operation, as well as a few that have been abandoned over the years. So much of the specialness of classic diners in Vermont is in the space itself, with abundant, shiny stainless steel or chrome; Formica countertops in fun colors and textures; unique, often geometric and brightly colored tile work; and the familiar throwback, nostalgic vibe that comes with it or is created from it.

Many diners are noted for their Art Deco design and retro flair, although each classic diner in Vermont really has its unique features and characteristics. When you are road-tripping throughout Vermont to these diners, the details of the interior spaces make the journey through time even more special. So many elements of the original diners in Vermont have withstood the test of time quite well and remain largely intact. Every diner—even if produced by the same manufacturer, largely Silk City Diners and Worcester Lunch Car Company diners—is wholly unique yet with similar characteristics to showcase the history and style of the premanufactured construction.

The barrel-roofed diner touts booth service, available in the original dining car inside the Chelsea Royal Diner.

THE BLUEPRINT OF A CLASSIC DINING CAR

One of the best ways to understand the structure of a premanufactured dining car is to study the blueprint of Ray's Diner, a dining car built in Fitchburg, Massachusetts, for Ray Beaudieu that now is home to the Windsor Diner in Windsor, Vermont. This blueprint, provided by current owner Theresa Taylor, shows the layout of how a traditional dining car was designed and built with particular finishes, along with the care and thought that went into its creation. This blueprint, dating back to July 2, 1952, shows the form and function of a traditional dining car and the ways in which its architecture would support the activity inside.

At the top of the blueprint for the Worcester Lunch Car Company dining car #835, the overall size for the dining car is noted: fifteen feet, six inches by thirty-six feet. Along the back wall of the building from left to right, a sixty-inch refrigerator is met by a forty-inch workbench, on which a "4-slice toastmaster" is placed. The exact location for the "Hotpoint fryer" is noted, along with a forty-two-inch counter for the Bain Marie, a container for hot water, used for slow cooking. Exhaust pipes even find their way into the blueprint. The right side of the manufacturing map shows another

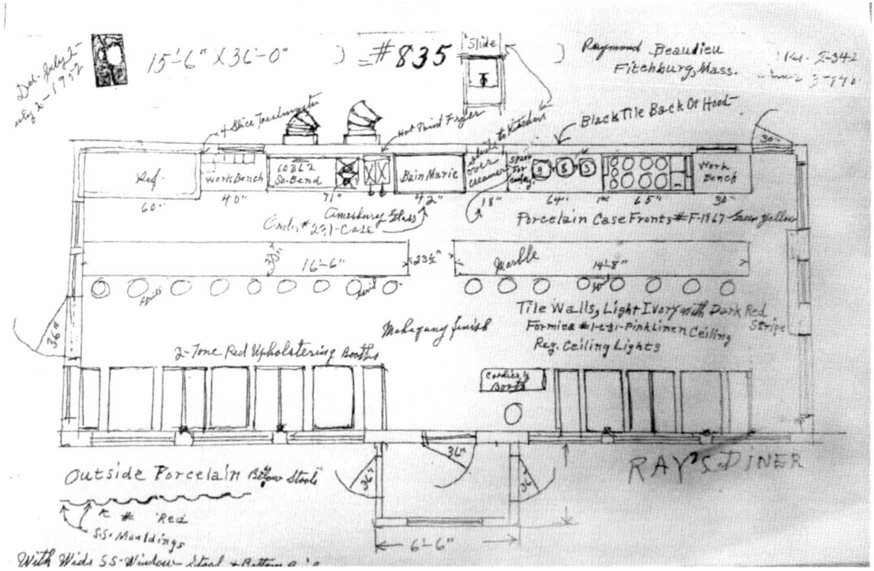

The original blueprint for the Windsor Diner shows the size, materials and original location of Fitchburg, Massachusetts. *Courtesy of Theresa Taylor.*

workspace, a sixty-five-inch flattop and a thirty-inch workbench. Specific finishes are noted as well; "2-tone red upholstering booths" and "mahogany finish" are written out, along with "tile walls, light ivory with dark red strip Formica #1-c-31-pink, linen ceiling and reg. ceiling lights," "black tile back of hood" and "Amesbury glass and porcelain case fronts #F-167." The thirty-inch-deep counter space has seventeen fixed stools, with an opening between the split counter of twenty-three and a half inches. The counter is marble. On the outside, "porcelain Bilou stools" are noted, along with "S.S. mouldings" and wide stainless-steel windows.

When visiting the Windsor Diner today after reviewing the blueprint, it's easy to see how the blueprint came to life in the dining car. The façade, sitting right on the roadside on Route 5 in Windsor, is wrapped with stainless-steel windows and red metal, accented by red-and-white striped flower boxes and the signature "Enjoy Coca-Cola" sign on top of the entrance above the green, white and black Windsor Diner sign.

Coupled with the blueprint is a "Cost Sheet for Construction of Diners," with copious notes and scribbles throughout this original piece of diner history. The structure is highly itemized with the material needs for the size of the car and the number of the car. Noted were the costs for steel for the platform,

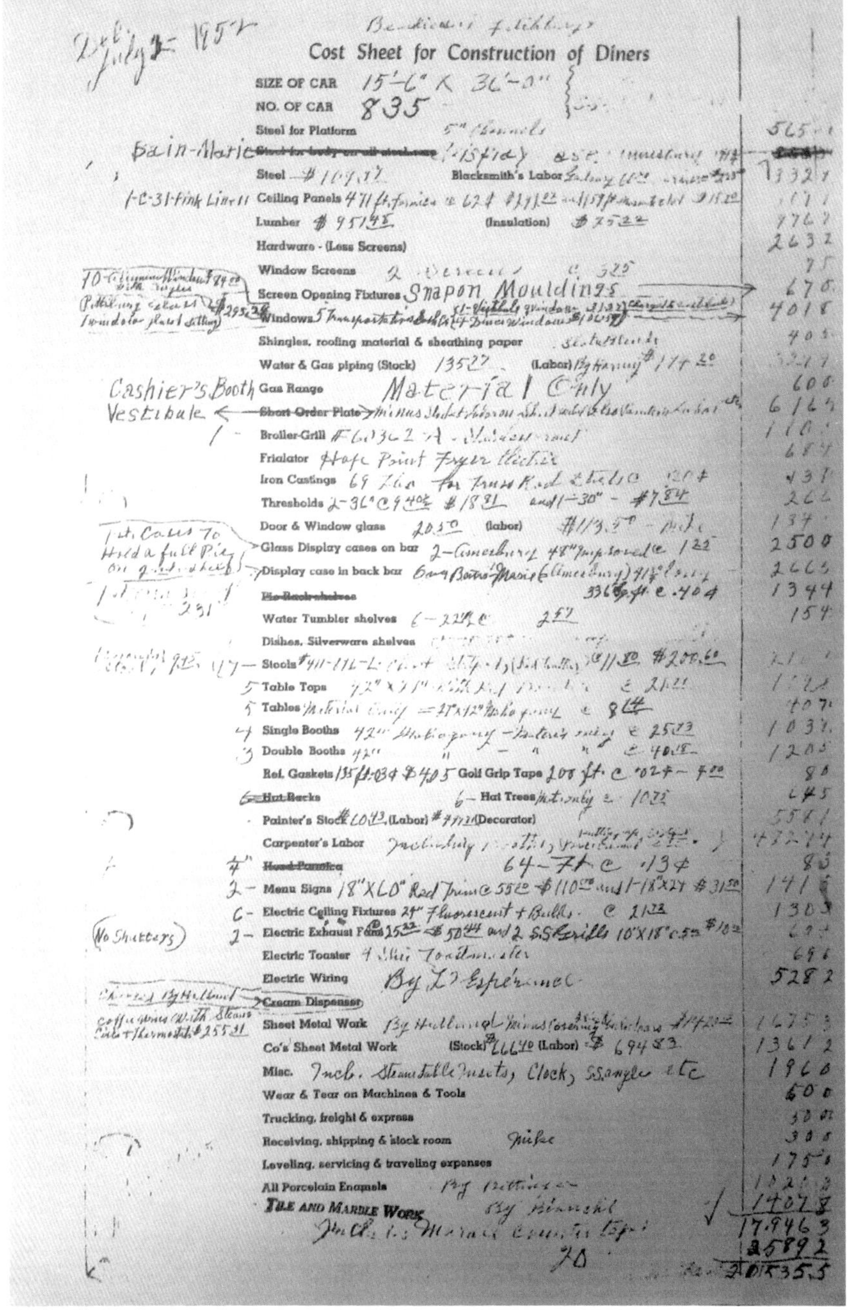

July 2 – 1952

Cost Sheet for Construction of Diners

SIZE OF CAR 15'-6" X 36'-0"

NO. OF CAR 835

Steel for Platform

Steel for body on all steel cars

Steel

Blacksmith's Labor

Ceiling Panels

Lumber

(Insulation)

Hardware - (Less Screens)

Window Screens

Screen Opening Fixtures Snapon Mouldings

Windows

Shingles, roofing material & sheathing paper

Water & Gas piping (Stock)

(Labor)

Gas Range Material Only

Short Order Plate

Broiler-Grill

Frialator

Iron Castings

Thresholds

Door & Window glass

(labor)

Glass Display cases on bar

Display case in back bar

Pie Rack shelves

Water Tumbler shelves

Dishes, Silverware shelves

Stools

Table Tops

Tables

Single Booths

Double Booths

Ref. Gaskets

Golf Grip Tape

Hat Racks

Hat Trees

Painter's Stock

(Labor)

(Decorator)

Carpenter's Labor

Hood Panels

Menu Signs

Electric Ceiling Fixtures

Electric Exhaust Fans

Electric Toaster

Electric Wiring

Cream Dispenser

Sheet Metal Work

Co's Sheet Metal Work

(Stock)

(Labor)

Misc.

Wear & Tear on Machines & Tools

Trucking, freight & express

Receiving, shipping & stock room

Leveling, servicing & traveling expenses

All Porcelain Enamels

TILE AND MARBLE WORK

A cost sheet outlines the necessary costs for the construction of diners in 1952. *Courtesy of Theresa Taylor.*

steel for the structure, the blacksmith's labor, the ceiling panels, lumber and insulation; hardware, window screens, screen opening fixtures (in this case, "snap-on mouldings"), windows, shingles, roofing material and sheathing paper; stock water and gas piping; cooking appliances, including a gas range, a broiler and grill and a Hotpoint Electric Fryer; iron castings, thresholds, door and window glass and a cashier's booth vestibule. Also outlined were the glass display cases on the bar, the display cases in the back bar, water tumbler shelves, dishes and silverware shelves. Out in front of the counter, seventeen stools, five tabletops, five tables, four single booths and three double booths were needed. Labor was included for the blacksmith, painters, sheet metal workers and carpenters. Menu signs were allocated for, along with six electric, fluorescent ceiling fixtures and two exhaust fans. Additionally, there were expenses included for wear and tear on machines and tools, trucking, freight and express, receiving, shipping and stock room, leveling, servicing and traveling. Porcelain enamel, tile work and marble work were additional expenses. Through one simple piece of paper, now a document of historical importance, a business was born and a classic diner erected.

SIGNAGE AT CLASSIC DINERS IN VERMONT

Signage at Vermont diners runs the gamut from the large roadside neon signs to hand-painted signs, such as at the Blue Benn in Bennington or Bob's in Manchester Center. The Blue Benn sign displayed across the front of the metal façade is complemented by the sign soaring high above. It is in fading blue letters in the same handwriting, positioned above an "Enjoy Coca-Cola" sign, as also seen at the Windsor Diner. Out back from the Blue Benn is another sign, hung on the painted-yellow cinder blocks of the exterior, that's a more polished and less homemade blue-and-yellow sign. The dining car itself at the Chelsea Royal Diner in Brattleboro highlights the words "Royal Diner," "Famous for Fine Food" and "Booth Service" in green block print, matching the green of the trim that accentuates the building, in addition to the large neon sign that's on the roadside. Like the Chelsea Royal, the Miss Bellows Falls in Bellows Falls also has its name prominently displayed across the front of the Worcester Lunch Company Car, with the words "Booth Service" noted on either side of the name. The Country Girl Diner's sign in Chester features the playful image of a young girl in pigtails with a feather sticking out of her mouth in a bright royal blue; this same iconic image of a country girl is depicted on the coffee mugs inside. The Diner's sign in Middlebury included a working clock so passersby were always aware of the time of day, similar to the clock found in the roadside sign and sign above the entrance at Bob's Diner in Manchester.

THE CLASSIC DINER'S EXTERIOR

The classic roadside diners in Vermont are long, narrow buildings that are primarily built of metal. They were prefabricated in a factory and trucked to their semipermanent or permanent locations; some of them have moved over time, but many have remained in their original drop locations. These traditional dining cars resemble and are often confused with actual railroad cars, but manufactured diners never rode the rails. They were designed solely for the purpose of being a cost-effective means for businesspeople to be served meals at affordable prices. In the late 1930s and 1940s, many dining cars were designed to carry the sleekness of the modern times. The classic dining cars in Vermont largely date from this period and must feature the rounded, elongated shape with copious metal on the façade. Some classic diners uniquely have barrel-vaulted ceilings, as seen in the Blue Benn in Bennington, Miss Bellows Falls in Bellows Falls and the Chelsea Royal Diner in Brattleboro. The Chelsea Royal Diner is a wonderful example of the softly curved, richly colored wooden ceiling, complemented by the wooden booths in the space. The barrel-vaulted ceilings are often best observed from the diner's exterior, where the rolling shape is seen most clearly.

Outside initially, many patrons of classic diners are drawn in through oversized neon signs, which are still seen at the Chelsea Royal Diner in Brattleboro, the Birdseye in Castleton and the Parkway Diner in South Burlington. The Blue Benn in Bennington had one originally, but it's since been removed. The neon signs that still remain immediately create a nostalgic, vintage feeling of time passed. They are an easy identifier of a classic diner in Vermont, of a diner institution. On the façade of the Birdseye Diner, the large orange neon sign sits over the metal roof and yellow-and-green trimmed structure. For the Parkway Diner, the antique sign with "Diner" lighting up sits tall between the street and the diner structure, announcing the diner's presence to those driving by. At the Chelsea Royal Diner, the neon sign is whimsical, depicting a goofy cartoon chef, accented by bright teal and yellow colors and lights, suspended by the side of the road. Henry's

Above: This is the truck that delivered the Country Girl Diner to Chester. *Courtesy of Jessica Holmes.*

Left: This truck driver delivered the Silk City Diner to Chester. *Courtesy of Jessica Holmes.*

This historical shot of Henry's Diner in Burlington, Vermont, shows the classic Vermont diner covered in snow. *Courtesy of Naomi Maglaris and John Couture.*

Diner, steps from Church Street in downtown Burlington, has a bright neon sign on a white background atop the entrance to the diner, complemented by signs boasting breakfast all day and gyros.

Over time, some diners, such as the Diner in Middlebury and the Miss Lyndonville Diner in Lyndonville, have evolved and expanded. And now, although the original dining car may no longer be outwardly visible, it is easy to identify the unique characteristics of its historic roots once inside. Many diners in Vermont have expanded their footprints with additions, such as the Birdseye in Castleton or Chelsea Royal Diner in Brattleboro, for capacity for guests. Others, like the Country Girl Diner in Chester, the Blue Benn in Bennington, Parkway Diner in South Burlington and Miss Bellows Falls in Bellows Falls, have kept their original footprints, largely preserving the original function of the spaces.

THE CLASSIC DINER'S INTERIOR

Inside, classic diners, much like mobile homes, have elongated, narrow interiors with long service or lunch counters with fixed, floor-mounted stools. Booth service is available in the front of the eatery, typically running the length of the diner against the windows. This combination of booths and sit-down counters is the defining configuration of a classic diner. Classic diners have colored tiled floors and backsplashes, stainless-steel panels above the counters and work areas and Formica countertops and tabletops, often with chrome metal trim.

Typically, there is a preparation area against the back wall, along with a flattop and griddle and perhaps also a fryer, a work station and a glass case for desserts. Many diners have built kitchen extensions or have relocated the line to the back of the diner to provide more space in the front of the house, as well as more room for their cooks to prepare meals quickly. One of the few diners where you can still interact with the line cooks as they're preparing your food is the Parkway Diner in South Burlington, where owner and chef Corey Gottfried will chat with you while whipping up your corned beef hash. Even the Parkway is now under another expansion for the line to move out back in the kitchen to allow the increasingly busy diner to find efficiency in food preparation.

Flattop grills, milkshake machines and soda fountains are staples of the classic diner, along with stainless-steel accessories throughout. The Country Girl Diner in Chester boasts an original lime-green Hamilton Beach milkshake maker down the far right of its counter. Glass cases protect sweet treats—from pies and cupcakes to cinnamon buns and scones—which are a staple at diners, along with a bottomless cup of coffee. Warm cups of joe are served often in a unique coffee mug that's reflective of the diner's own brand.

Some diners, including the Blue Benn in Bennington and the Parkway Diner in South Burlington, also feature stained-glass windows in the interior, adding to the charm and character of the space. In the Blue Benn, the geometric glass with blue, teal and yellow panes depicts coffee and pie and coffee, eggs and toast—diner staples. At the Parkway Diner, a stained-glass depiction in teal, gray and yellow showcases the diner itself.

When visiting the classic diners of Vermont, compare and contrast the exteriors and interior spaces to witness the passage of time and begin to identify the subtle differences between the manufacturers of these dining cars. Much of the rich history is preserved through the classic diner characteristics. Design elements remain unchanged over time in Vermont's diners, similar to the role the diner still plays in the community it serves.

Chapter 4

CHELSEA ROYAL DINER

(802) 254-8399
487 Marlboro Road
Brattleboro, Vermont 05301
chelsearoyaldiner.com

AN INTRODUCTION TO BRATTLEBORO AND THE CHELSEA ROYAL DINER

Brattleboro, Vermont, is a gateway town from Massachusetts into Vermont located in Windham County. Originally Brattleborough, the eastern Vermont town borders the Connecticut River and was chartered in 1753. Historically, Brattleboro was known as a mill town, having a gristmill, sawmill, woolen textile mill and paper mill at one point. Now, the town is well traveled by tourists and locals alike as a main corridor to southern Vermont. The town is rich in arts and education, featuring the Vermont Jazz Center, New England Center for Circus Arts and three college campuses: SIT Graduate Institute, John Wollman College and Marlboro College Graduate School. Brattleboro has also become a destination in Vermont for its craft brewery (Hermit Thrush), its covered bridge (the Creamery Covered Bridge) and extensive hiking, biking and ski trails in close vicinity.

Located on a busy road leading to ski country off Interstate 91 in southern Vermont, the Chelsea Royal Diner in West Brattleboro is a popular spot for

Next to the Chelsea Royal Diner is an ice cream stand, complete with homemade ice cream in the warmer months.

breakfast, lunch and dinner. The roadside eatery is also known to draw in families driving by for homemade ice cream and Vermont creemees—soft-serve ice cream—in the warmer months. Ice cream is available all year round for pies a la mode, sundaes, floats and milkshakes. The location is a few miles outside downtown Brattleboro, where the dining car was originally located. Patrons are diverse, from truck drivers and local businesspeople to college students and retirees. It's also a popular spot for tourists who are lured in by the bright and colorful neon roadside sign and massive ice cream cone marking the property. From the road, it's one of the most eye-catching and attractive diners that embodies the vintage vibe for which diners are known. The restaurant houses a total of sixty seats, serves three meals a day and is open for fifteen hours a day, from 5:30 a.m. to 9:00 p.m. The Chelsea Royal Diner is one of few Vermont diners that still serves dinner and is open in the evening hours. It is well loved by locals and travelers, dishing up nearly three hundred meals a day, with roughly 40 percent of products sourced locally.

The Chelsea Royal Diner is proud to be part of the Vermont Fresh Network, a community of "agricultural and culinary professionals that use Vermont grown and raised foods to create economic, environmental, and social gain." To qualify for the Vermont Fresh Network designation, restaurant chefs need to pledge that a certain amount of annual food purchases will be Vermont grown or produced. A certain portion of food must be purchased from Vermont Fresh Network farmers and chef partners. The Chelsea Royal Diner is rooted in buying local and being environmentally conscious. In fact, the diner has been composting for a number of years and serving up only grass-fed beef, butchered from a whole steer from neighboring Winterview Farm in Springfield. All of its "veal, steaks, burgers, ground beef, and grilled liver are from local, grass-fed beef," as the menu touts and celebrates. Out behind the building is Royal Farm, the diner's own garden. With two large vegetable gardens over three acres, the diner sources local seasonal ingredients for its kitchen, including the homepage pickles and backyard eggs. This locally driven focus of the Chelsea Royal Diner largely embodies the Vermont brand and hyper-local focus.

THE HISTORY OF THE CHELSEA ROYAL DINER

Janet Picard and Todd Darrah have owned the Chelsea Royal Diner and the neighboring ice cream stand since 1990. Prior to purchasing the diner, Darrah worked at a French restaurant in Ridgefield, Connecticut, and then seven years at the Hermitage Club in Wilmington, Vermont, followed by starting his own restaurant in Wilmington. The diner itself is a 1939 Worcester Lunch Car Company dining car (#736). In the 1980s, the Royal Diner car, known as the Royal Yard Restaurant at one time, sat off the road near the intersection of Route 5 and Route 9 in Brattleboro. Darrah ended up finding the rundown dining car and moved it to its current location in 1987. It was restored into the well-loved eatery it is now where it currently sits. The original sign for the diner popped up in 1999 at a barn in New Hampshire and was revamped and reinstalled on the site, drawing in travelers by the road. The building next door, built to expand the space, dates to 1950. Many of the employees have been with the restaurant as long as Picard and Darrah, adding to the community history and family-like atmosphere of the diner.

THE AMBIANCE AT THE CHELSEA ROYAL DINER

Driving up to the roadside restaurant, the green words of "Royal Diner," "Famous for Fine Food" and "Booth Service" pop against the green trim that accentuates the dining car's traditional lines. From the exterior, notice the barrel-vaulted ceiling and the metal elements. Step inside the Chelsea Royal Diner and you'll walk into the addition. Step to the left, and you'll find a well-loved and well-aged round dining car, complete with a wooden ceiling and sturdy wooden booths. The barrel-vaulted roof is tied to the newer addition, which allowed the location to expand and seat more than sixty people at a time. The windows and double front doors are original, along with the counter stools that were moved to the main dining room and the coolers out back.

Inside the Chelsea Royal Diner, you'll see warm colors and walls, complemented by bright-colored, abstract nature paintings created by Picard herself. The diner's original counter was removed and reinstalled in the expanded restaurant next to the dining car. On the counter, you'll find a tray of oversized cinnamon buns covered in icing, ready to be scooped up or taken to go. The green booths in the addition, along with yellow walls, pink tabletops and worn wooden floors, are accented by green and brass lamps. These unique elements add to the warm interior that is immediately inviting. In the dining car itself, the intricately tiled blue-and-white floor remains, showing some signs of age. There are wooden elements in the barreled ceiling and wooden booths that resemble the shapes of pews and wooden tables. Inside, a sign dates the space to April 12, 1939, immediately conveying to visitors the rich history of the space in which they're dining.

FOOD AND BEVERAGE AT THE CHELSEA ROYAL DINER

Clean, high-end homestyle cuisine is how the Chelsea Royal touts its affordable fare, with homemade ingredients and locally sourced products as much as possible. Hand-cut fries, gravy made from beef bones, homemade pesto sourced with basil from the garden and, of course, homemade ice cream are just a few examples of the home cooking that happens at the Chelsea Royal Diner. Coffee is poured freely into classic, thick-handled diner mugs that display a modernized logo that's a take on the neon roadside sign. The menu reflects that logo design and the sign out front in an eye-catching format that instantly reminds you you're in a historic location, with the 1939 date at the top of the menu. Gluten-free, vegetarian and vegan options are plentiful at the Chelsea Royal and denoted on the menu. Diners have historically been accommodating to guests, modifying meals to make exactly what a patron requests. Working with diner patrons with allergies and food preferences is a direction in which many Vermont diners are going as well.

Breakfast is served all day at the Chelsea Royal Diner, with signature dishes including the Chesapeake Bay Benedict, with crab cakes, poached eggs and hollandaise; Pancakes, with the choice of apple-cinnamon, banana, blueberry or chocolate chip; or, for the seriously hungry, the Royal Feast, a half Belgian short stack of pancakes, two eggs any style, bacon, ham and hash browns. A range of omelets, including the Spanish Omelet (peppers, onions and spicy tomato sauce), the Mushroom and Cheese Omelet, the Western Omelet, the Popeye Omelet (mushrooms and Swiss cheese topped with sour cream and black olives) and the Vermont Omelet (cheddar cheese, bacon and green onions), are a popular selection served alongside raisin toast or sunflower wheat bread. The homemade Cinnamon Buns, oozing with frosting, are a must whether eating in or taking out.

The Chelsea Royal is one of few classic diners in Vermont serving dinners and still embracing the blue plate special—that is, meat, starch and vegetables served traditionally on a blue plate with three separations for the three main components of the meal, served with a choice of salad or soup. At the Chelsea Royal, these two-course square meals range in price from $9.99 to $13.99. Some days are themed, such as Wednesdays with Italian fare and Fridays with fresh seafood.

Blue plate special menu offerings include:

Monday (Onion Soup or Salad)
Pan-Fried Chicken, with mashed potatoes, gravy and choice of vegetable
New England Boiled Dinner
Char-grilled Sirloin Tips, with sautéed mushrooms and onions

Tuesday (Cream of Mushroom Soup or Salad)
Turkey Croquettes
Grass-Fed Chopped Sirloin Steak, eight ounces, charbroiled with mushroom gravy
Boiled Ham Dinner, New England style

Wednesday (Tomato Basil Bisque or Salad)
Veal Parmesan with spaghetti and garlic bread
Baked Ziti, made with four cheeses and garlic bread
Baked Manicotti, made with three cheeses and garlic bread

Thursday (Black Bean Soup or Salad)
Chicken-Fried Pork
French Dip with au jus and French fries
Braised Lamb Shank

Friday (New England Clam Chowder or Salad)
Fish Fry with French fries and coleslaw
Maryland Crab Cakes with French fries and coleslaw
Fried Clam Strip Platter with French fries and coleslaw

Saturday (Cream of Broccoli Soup or Salad)
Chicken Potpie with fresh melon
Baked Stuffed Chicken Breast
Chicken-Fried Steak with country gravy

Sunday (Split Pea Soup or Salad)
Yankee Pot Roast, New England style
Roast Leg of Lamb
Mexican Special

Chelsea Royal Diner's menu is extensive and not limited to the stick-to-your-ribs type of fare. Although you will find traditional diner meals like Grilled Liver and Onions, Boiled Dinners, BLTs and Open-Faced Turkey Sandwiches, there are ample Italian dishes, fish and seafood platters, pizzas and a complete Mexican menu available Friday and Saturday nights, including nachos and quesadillas, burritos, chimichangas, taco platters, taco salads and fajitas. Also on Fridays, the diner serves its "famous" Prime Rib and Fish Fries. This diverse menu with a wide range of signature cuisines showcases Darrah's well-rounded ability as a chef and the delicate art of balancing innovation with history, especially in a setting so rooted in how it used to be.

Guest favorites at the Chelsea Royal Diner include Brattleboro's Best Buffalo Wings; a 100 percent Bison Cheddar Burger, made with local pasture-raised bison; a Reuben with all the traditional fixings; Macaroni and Cheese served with a foot-long Hot Dog and Vermont cheddar; Mom's Meatloaf; a Teriyaki Chicken Breast dinner; and the Fried Clam Roll. Seafood in Vermont is a thing? It is at the Chelsea Royal Diner. The diner prides itself on getting some of the freshest seafood in New England regularly.

A colorful board boasting a variety of homemade desserts adorns a wall in the Chelsea Royal Diner. Apple pie, raspberry pie, maple walnut pie, lemon meringue pie, carrot cake, chocolate pudding, Indian pudding, tapioca and bread pudding all appeal to diner-goers' sweet tooths at the end of the meal, or perhaps to start it. The Chelsea Royal serves up hard ice cream, creemees and frozen yogurt and offers ice cream sundaes with hot fudge, real whipped cream and a cherry on top, of course. The classically prepared Banana Split is a favorite, along with the Maple Walnut Pie sundae. You can even get a hand-packed ice cream pint to go. Picnic tables outside in the summertime are always full with families dropping by for a sweet summer treat from the iconic roadside stop that's become a destination for locals and tourists in Vermont's gateway town.

Chapter 5

COUNTRY GIRL DINER

(802) 875-1003
46 Vermont Route 103
Chester, Vermont 05143
countrygirldiner.com

INTRODUCTION TO CHESTER AND THE COUNTRY GIRL DINER

Chester, located in southeastern Vermont in Windsor County, was originally chartered in 1754 and then rechartered in 1761. Covering fifty-six square miles, the town is served by Vermont Route 103, Vermont Route 11, Vermont Route 10 and Vermont Route 35. Chester is located close to some of Vermont's best ski areas, including Okemo, Killington, Bromley, Magic Mountain, Mount Snow and Stratton, which bring tourists through the quiet and charming southern Vermont town. The population of Chester is just over three thousand residents strong, according to the town's website (MeetChesterVermont.com). Chester is truly the epitome of an authentic Vermont town, with more dirt roads than paved roads—where life is simple and the locals like it that way. Chester is the exemplar of what small-town life should be in Vermont. The town green in Chester acts as a central meeting space and a focal point for the town. Chester is most well known for its Stone Village Historic District and the Chester Village History District, both of which are recognized in the National Register of Historic Places. The quaint town has a mixture of Victorian and Greek architecture and is accented by stone from local quarries. Locally owned gift shops—including Sage Jewelry and Gifts, DaVallia Art and Accents and Country on The Common—and the Stone House Antique Center and Vermont Institute of Contemporary Arts help root Chester in art, history and culture.

Set along Route 103 South in Chester, the Country Girl Diner has played a vital role in the community since the 1960s. It's the "soul of the community," according to Jessica Holmes, the current owner of the historic dining car. The diner truly is a gathering place in town and where the locals come together for conversation and to share news. Now, the welcoming roadside eatery is open seven days a week for breakfast and lunch and includes Friday night Prime Rib dinners, serving up house-made barbecue ribs and beer-battered fish from 5:00 p.m. to 8:00 p.m. in the summertime. The diner also hosts Cruise-in Car Shows, where those patrons who show up with a classic car receive 10 percent off their dinner meal. These events bring community members and tourists together and celebrate their common ground over big portions of food made with care. "Great food and great friends. That's what

The welcoming entrance to the Country Girl Diner in Chester is flanked by artsy cows on each side.

we're all about" is Country Girl's motto. The diner is open for breakfast and lunch from 7:00 a.m. to 2:30 p.m., Monday through Saturday, and 7:00 a.m. to 2:00 p.m. on Sunday, when it features all-day breakfast. Like many Vermont diners, the Country Girl is cash only, with an ATM on-site.

THE HISTORY OF THE COUNTRY GIRL DINER

The Country Girl Diner is a 1944 Silk City dining car, built by the Paterson Vehicle Company in Paterson, New Jersey. The owners think the dining car is one of few surviving examples of the Silk City dining cars from that time. The diner has been in its present location on Route 103 South since 1966, after a brief stay in Jaffrey, New Hampshire. From Jaffrey, it was trucked to Chester and has remained in its current spot since. According to current owner Holmes, "Just before the diner was brought to Chester, Dooley's owned the building but leased the land. When the landlord raised the lease for property, Dooley took his building to the other end of town that night to a spot now known as Salon 2000." In March 2017, current owners Holmes and husband and chef Paul Frasca purchased the diner from Kate and Thom Huntington, who had owned the diner since 2011. Holmes and Frasca had largely grown up in the food business, so it made perfect sense for the Huntingtons to pass along the diner when they relocated out of state. "Kate is an artist and wanted to move on and open a store in Maryland," Holmes explained. "We always loved the diner. From the day we started working there, we knew we wanted to own it. Paul actually said his very first day that he worked at the Country Girl that someday he would own it. And here we are now. We couldn't be happier," Holmes shared.

Frasca graduated from New Hampshire Culinary Institute before working at restaurants on Lake George in New York State and at Okemo in Vermont, while Holmes is a self-taught baker. Holmes explained, "Paul was the cook. I was a waitress and cook at the Country Girl before we purchased it. I did a lot of prep and baking. I was doing a little bit of everything, really. Before the diner, previously I always had an office job as a bookkeeper and administrator. I also ran a landscaping company on the side and did some waitressing on the weekends. We've both been in the restaurant business since we were teenagers. This was the right next step."

For Holmes and Frasca, who have more than seventy years of combined experience working in the restaurant business, owning and operating the

The roadside Dooley Diner was also located in Chester, Vermont. *Courtesy of Jessica Holmes.*

A historical photo of the Country Girl shows its original roadside appearance. *Courtesy of Jessica Holmes.*

Country Girl Diner allowed the couple to have more family time with their four kids, two of whom are grown. Holmes recounted, "We always worked at night until midnight or two o'clock in the morning. The diner allows us to have our evenings together as a family." Two of their four kids also help in the diner. Frasca's son Zach, twenty-three, is a cook at the diner. Zach and Frasca work together 90 percent of the time, with Holmes cooking on the line one day a week. Otherwise, she's waitressing, baking—sometimes with her eleven-year-old daughter, who comes in to help—or bookkeeping.

Former owner Kate Huntington remarked, "I love this diner with every ounce of my being and am so proud of the next level that Jess and Paul have taken it to. I poured my life into saving it from disrepair, and when we sold it to them, I felt like there were no other people we would hand ownership over to." Huntington continued, "They have kept the same menu and staff and have just upped the ante on what they send out of the kitchen. They are wonderful, and this place is magic—the customers as well as the staff!"

THE AMBIANCE AT THE COUNTRY GIRL DINER

The first thing you notice when pulling up to the Country Girl Diner are the two artsy cow heads flanking the main entrance, along with an "OPEN" sign and American flag. The big blue sign above the door with a country girl wearing pigtails immediately brings you back to simpler times. This same playful caricature makes her way onto the coffee cups found inside. In the summer, flower boxes overflowing with color add warmth to the façade and show genuine care and pride of ownership. There's also an outdoor deck and picnic tables for enjoying meals al fresco in the warmer Vermont months.

Inside the tiny Silk City Diner, with only sixteen stools at the counter and six booths, the vintage décor is accented by modern touches. Red stools, worn wooden footrests and red-and-white booth cushions give the space a homey vibe in stark contrast to gleaming stainless steel behind the counter. The mosaic, black-and-white tiled floor—original to the diner, along with the footrests—adds character and contrasts the warmer wooden touches. On the far counter to the right is a soft green Hamilton Beach milkshake maker—original to the diner. A red banner hangs to the left of the dining car with the simple word "Love," with which the diner is filled by the warmth and welcoming nature of the waitstaff and the tasty creations coming out of the kitchen.

Holmes and Frasca, along with the Huntingtons before them, have strived to keep as much as possible in the building original. If something has been replaced or needs to be, they'll try to source something that's authentic to the era of their Silk City dining car. They want to preserve the historical feel of the space in order to distinguish their special diner from modern eateries. Holmes said, "I love what it is and what it was originally. I'll leave it as original as possible." Previously, there was a line out front to cook, but there has always been a kitchen out back as well. In front, they've kept the appearance as close to the original as possible. The countertops have been replaced, along with new metal-rimmed Formica tables.

FOOD AND BEVERAGE AT THE COUNTRY GIRL DINER

Simple, real food is what you'll find at the Country Girl, with creative twists and locally sourced Vermont products whenever possible, such as Cabot Creamery butter and real maple syrup for pancakes, of course. The Country Girl Diner "serves a helping of love with every plate," which is a testament to the love owner Holmes shows her staff and patrons. For breakfast, cage-free eggs from Maple Meadow Farm are made into traditional breakfast platters and custom omelets. Many of the dishes feature local Vermont names, such as the Killington Classic (a French toast sandwich with two fried eggs, bacon and a side of maple syrup) or the Stratton Scramble, with seasoned black beans, onions, scrambled eggs and Vermont cheddar. The Stowe is two farm-fresh scrambled eggs on a grilled buttered bulkie with Vermont cheddar cheese and choice of ham, bacon or a sausage patty. Some dishes, like the Bromley Burrito, have a Mexican flair, with seasoned black beans, farm-fresh scrambled eggs, sausage, tomatoes, onions, salsa and Vermont cheddar in a grilled flour tortilla. The Country Girl serves up bottomless cups of New England Coffee Company coffee, along with hot chocolate with Cabot whipped cream and milkshakes from their original milkshake machine, available in vanilla, chocolate or strawberry.

For lunch, foot-long hot dogs come with a variety of toppings, from grilled peppers and onions to Thousand Island dressing, sauerkraut and mustard. The Country BLT is stacked high on robust Texas toast with a huge pile of potato chips and a pickle or hand-cut fries, sweet potato fries or onion rings. The Grilled Tuna Melt is served on marbled rye with Swiss cheese, and the Soup and Sandwich Special with grilled cheese and tomato chowder is a popular comfort food. With seven burgers on the menu made daily, there's a burger for everyone, along with a Tuna Salad Platter, Chicken Tenders Platter and Cheesesteak and Fries platter. The Smash Burger, made with 100 percent ground beef, is a popular choice. Onions are smashed into the patties, and they caramelize as the burger cooks. To finish it off, the burger is topped with Swiss and hand-cut fries. Gluten-free bread and buns are available to accommodate all patrons and their dietary preferences.

The desserts take center stage when seated at the counter, which runs the length of the diner. With just the right hint of sweetness, the Maple Walnut Pie with a generous dab of whipped cream is a staple, along with Key Lime Pie, a Chocolate Chip Cookie Skillet, Chocolate Mousse Cake, Pumpkin Pie and Apple Pie. Vermont maple syrup from Mitch's located right in Chester, less than a mile from the diner, is available for purchase on-site by the quart or pint.

According to owner Holmes, the Country Girl is best known for "our homemade corned beef hash and French toast specialties like Boston Cream or Coconut Cream French Toast. Big beautiful burgers with onion rings on top and hand-cut fries or sandwich melts on big Texas bread are a few lunch faves. Chicken Potpie—it's like Grandma makes. We come from big Italian families, so food is so important to us and part of who we are," Holmes laughed. Desserts are very popular as well, as in most classic diners. Holmes shared, "We have a lot of people order just dessert or dessert first, and we sell to Okemo Mountain year-round." The food keeps people coming back, but "everyone feels included in conversation and the feel of the place," Holmes said. "Everyone is happy to be here. Everyone loves coming and seeing people. You always have someone to talk to. That's important especially; it just feels good."

The Role of the Country Girl Diner in the Local Community

"I feel like the Country Girl is the soul of the community," Holmes said. "Everyone comes together. There are many people who don't have much else going on. We see people every day who are looking for a friendly face and a good bite to eat. We're all friends. Really, we're all family. Everyone is welcome. We just love that." There are generations of people coming back to the Country Girl, and everyone seems to have a story about the diner or a memory about how it's played a role in their lives. Holmes shared that the family who owned the diner when it was in its prior location in Jaffrey, New Hampshire, came to see it in its new location. Together, they shared memories and enjoyed a meal, with the diner serving as the common thread between their lives and families.

The Country Girl serves a lot of the same locals in Chester every day. For some regulars, the waitresses know exactly what he or she will order on any given day. For others, they can even see them parking and have their meal nearly ready when they walk through the door. In fact, they have one customer who comes in every day for breakfast. He's the first in the door and then comes every day for lunch as well. The diner has roughly thirty people who come in for coffee or a meal every single morning, according to Holmes. One morning, a regular didn't show up for breakfast. One of the waitresses went to his home to check on him since he doesn't have anyone at home. The waitresses at the Country Girl truly care about their patrons' well-being. According to Holmes, "These people are part of our family now. We really get attached to these people. The hardest thing has been to lose some of our regulars. They really are your family, even if you don't know them that well. I just love what we do and the people we serve so much." The Country Girl Diner hosts customer appreciation nights in an effort to say thank you to the people who support the diner and its staff in the slower times of the year. According to Holmes, these people largely keep the diner alive and thriving.

In terms of what's to come for the future of the Country Girl Diner, Holmes doesn't anticipate any changes. She thinks it will continue to grow, with more people stopping and making it a destination, but for the predictable future, the Country Girl Diner will continue to bring locals and tourists together in a central meeting place in the quaint town of Chester.

Chapter 6

THE BLUE BENN DINER

(802) 442-5140
314 North Street,
Bennington, Vermont, 05201

AN INTRODUCTION TO BENNINGTON AND THE BLUE BENN DINER

Bennington, in Bennington County in southern Vermont, is one of two shire towns in the county and the second-largest town in the Green Mountain State. It is surrounded by New York State to the west and the Vermont towns of Pownal, Shaftsbury and Woodford. The town is home to more than fifteen thousand residents. Bennington was settled in 1761, at which point there were three (now historic) districts composing the town: North Bennington, downtown Bennington and Old Bennington. During the Revolutionary War, the Battle of Bennington took place in the town. Bennington is perhaps most well known as the home to the Bennington Battle Monument, the tallest man-made structure in Vermont at 306 feet, erected in 1891. The town is also well known and regarded for its role in manufacturing iron, textiles and pottery, along with wood processing. Bennington is also home to a number of colleges, including Bennington College and Southern Vermont College, both four-year liberal arts colleges, along with the Northeastern Baptist College, the Community College of Vermont and Vermont Technical College.

Today, the historic downtown area boasts a variety of businesses, from bakeries and cafés to art stores and galleries, museums, breweries, boutiques and more attractions. Tourists looking to take in the rich history of Bennington often visit the Bennington Battle Monument and the Bennington Battlefield State Historic Site, the Bennington Museum, the Park-McCullough Historic House, the Wilson Castle, the Silk Road Covered Bridge and the Burt Henry Covered Bridge. The arts also thrive in Bennington, as the home to the Bennington Center for the Arts, the Bennington Arts Guild Gallery, Bennington Potters, Vermont Arts Exchange, the Chamber Music Conference and Composer's Forum to the East. Outdoor recreation includes the Molly Stark Trail for a forty-mile scenic drive between Bennington and Brattleboro, along with Harmon Hill for hiking. In a town steeped in history, culture, art and education, it's fitting that the Blue Benn Diner continues to play such a fundamental role in the community as a gathering place for locals, visitors and college students.

THE HISTORY OF THE BLUE BENN DINER

The menu at the Blue Benn Diner, also known as Sonny's Blue Benn, tells the story of the iconic roadside eatery in Bennington. It reads, "You are about to experience a treat as uncommon as the institution you are now in...the great American diner. Look around you. You are surrounded by history. The Blue Benn Diner is a Silk City creation, prefabricated in New Jersey in the 1940's. Note the frequency of stainless steel, the barreled ceiling, the proximity of the kitchen, and the fabulous design of the railroad dining car. If the motif intrigues you, wait 'til you try the food! History is now! The choices offered on this menu are fresh-cooked, piping hot, and suit the aura of a fast vanishing time when good food and fair prices put America on the Road."

The diner itself is a 1948 Silk City Diner manufactured by Paterson Vehicle Company of Paterson, New Jersey. In 1948, it was shipped and assembled at its current location in Bennington and hasn't moved since. The Monroe family purchased it in 1974 after the previous owner decided to close up the classic diner. At that time, the grill moved from the front of the diner into the back of the kitchen.

THE AMBIANCE AT THE BLUE BENN DINER

From the outside of the Blue Benn Diner, the classic dining car is almost disguised by bright blue awnings in the front of the property. Peering beyond the blue awnings, however, visitors see extensive stainless steel and ample windows lining the dining car. A hand-painted sign atop an "Enjoy Coca-Cola" sign allows visitors to see the diner from quite a distance, while another sign in blue cursive over a white background appears above the main entrance to the classic diner. Yet another sign in blue and yellow appears on the back of the building. Originally when the Monroes purchased the diner, there was a neon sign that, due to local ordinances, they had to take down.

When you step into the Blue Benn Diner, the blue from the exterior carries through into the interior space. Counter stools alternate in aqua blue and white, while light blue tiles with a black border line the counter. The counter shows the diner's age and the rich history of many meals served to guests seated at the counter. You can literally see the elbow prints in the worn Formica. Behind the counter, menu items appear on pastel pieces of paper—green, pink, blue and yellow in plastic sleeves—advertising meals to enjoy at the Blue Benn along with a handwritten specials board. Some of the menu items displayed are handwritten, others are typed—all are hung with tape seemingly decorating the space. Functioning Stereophonic jukeboxes

The hand-painted sign for the Blue Benn in Bennington matches the handwritten menus found inside.

operated by quarters sit at every table, a rarity among other classic diners in Vermont. Songs like Bruce Springsteen's "Born in the USA," the Righteous Brothers' "Unchained Melody," Elvis Presley's "Hound Dog," the Supremes' "You Can't Hurry Love" and Buddy Holly's "Oh Boy" bring guests back to simpler times. Twenty-five cents buys you two songs. Low-backed booths line the entrance against the windows with colorful cushions, matching the menu items hanging behind the counter. The floor is well-worn tile. Two stained-glass windows appear on either side of the dining car—one depicting a hearty breakfast of eggs, toast and coffee and the other showing a cup of coffee and a big slice of pie (likely cherry) among a geometric backdrop of greens, yellows and varying shades of blue. These stained-glass windows are a draw for visitors, in addition to the food. Much of the interior remains untouched. The only real addition has been the entryway and awnings to keep the often-harsh weather of Vermont off diner-goers inside.

Due to the popularity of the roadside eatery and its small size, rules are laid out on the front door: "Please be seated in this waiting area. A waitress will call you when a booth is cleared and ready. No need to give name—Use honor system. You may sit at any available counter space. However, you will lose your place in line for a booth if you sit at the counter." The rules are obeyed by regulars and tourists alike, showing respect to the historic diner and the workers inside. The interior of the classic diner is tight and always packed, which also creates a distinct energy and sense of community in the space.

FOOD AND BEVERAGE AT THE BLUE BENN DINER

There is nearly always a line at the popular roadside eatery, with folks waiting for the call for the next available booth. The cash-only diner has only forty-some seats and hasn't gone through an expansion like many classic diners in Vermont have to increase their capacities. The Blue Benn is open from 6:00 a.m. to 8:00 p.m. daily. The Monroe family has been serving a mixture of traditional diner fare and more innovative dishes since 1974. The menu is one of the most unique of all Vermont's classic diners and accommodates a range of dietary restrictions and preferences, offering egg substitutes, gluten-free bread and many variations of traditional dishes. In fact, there's even a "Veggie Corner" on the menu, which includes Veggie Chili with jalapeño corn bread, a Marinated Portabella Mushroom, a

Shiitake Mushroom and Broccoli Stir Fry, a Veggie Meatloaf with garden gravy, a Nut Burger, Falafels, an Eggplant-Almond Enchilada and a Veggie Burrito. The vegetarian dishes are hearty and extensive, adding to the diner's accommodating nature.

Serving breakfast all day, Sonny's Blue Benn is known for its variety of pancakes, including Blueberry, Blueberry Almond, Whole Wheat, Whole Wheat Harvest with a mix of berries, Whole Wheat Apple or Cranberry Apple, Crunch Berry with raspberries and granola, Multi-Grain with blueberries, Multi-Grain with cranberries and nuts, Banana Walnut and their Grandson Matheson's Chocolate Chip Raspberry pancakes, all ranging from $4.25 to $5.95 for a big platter of fluffy pancakes. More than sixteen omelets are available on the breakfast menu as well, served with toast and substitutions of Egg Beaters or egg whites. The Philly Cheese omelet features shaved steak, peppers, onions, mushrooms and cheese, while the Sir Benn, a locals' favorite, features chicken, broccoli, mushrooms, cheese and hollandaise. Other specialty omelets include Apple Cheddar, Greek (with feta, tomatoes, onions and spices), Asparagus and Cheddar, Spinach and Sour Cream, Shiitake Mushroom and Broccoli and Salmon with sour cream and dill.

Lunch specials include Hot Open-Faced Sandwiches, with your choice of hamburger, roast beef or turkey, with mashed or French fries and a vegetable, served on white bread with homemade gravy. Club sandwiches are another crowd favorite, available with a choice of ham, turkey, roast beef or hamburger. Dinner specials include Chicken Picatta; Pot Roast of Beef; Real Roasted Turkey with homemade dressing and cranberry sauce, your choice of dark meat or all-white meat; one-half Fried Chicken with Spaghetti; Baked Meatloaf; Grilled Liver and Onions with Bacon; and a variety of seafood, from Fried Haddock Filet to Fried Shrimp, Fried Scallops and a Fisherman's Platter. Dessert at the Blue Benn features Homemade Indian Pudding and Hot Fudge Pudding Cake, both served warm with a scoop of vanilla ice cream; Tapioca Pudding; Pumpkin Bread Pudding; pies; crisps; and ice cream.

The menu also reads a sincere word of thanks from the owners, Sonny, Marylou, Lisa and staff, saying, "Please accept our appreciation and sincere thanks for letting us serve you—sometimes in the rush of business life, we fail to say—THANKS—loud enough but you can be sure. Your patronage is never taken for granted. To serve you is a privilege and a pleasure."

THE ROLE OF THE BLUE BENN IN THE LOCAL COMMUNITY

The Blue Benn is home to many locals and students in the area and has become a draw for tourists as well. Cheyanne Forgatch, from Mullica Hill, New Jersey, shared, "I know Blue Benn has been around for quite a number of years and is deeply loved by the community. The people are always so nice and welcoming. We were there for the first time about twelve or so years ago. I just love how the menu is handwritten on the wall. The pumpkin pancakes are my favorite, but the hash is really good too. After the time being there, we now go out of our way to stop!"

Jane Swift, former governor of Massachusetts, who has been frequenting the diner for over twenty-five years, shared, "Our whole family loves the Blue Benn. Between my husband who is a vegetarian, my gluten allergy and three fussy kids, that is hard to find!" She continued to talk about the waitstaff, which is part of the diner's appeal and keeps people going back. Swift said, "The service at the Blue Benn is efficient and friendly. The same waitstaff has been there for years! As for food, some of our family favorites are the home fries, the grilled corn muffin and the omelets, which are always perfect—fluffy, with plenty of filling and never runny. And they have gluten-free toast! Not to mention the chocolate chip pancakes for the kiddos. And bring quarters for the individualized jukebox selections at each table—oldies. Also, always bring cash. Never seat yourself at a booth—wait in the foyer area. These are all strict rules." For all visitors, the combination of these "diner rules," the unchanged atmosphere and the ample offerings create a dining experience hard to find elsewhere in Vermont.

Chapter 7

MISS BELLOWS FALLS DINER

(802) 463-3700
90 Rockingham Street
Bellows Falls, Vermont 05101

AN INTRODUCTION TO BELLOWS FALLS AND THE MISS BELLOWS FALLS DINER

Bellows Falls is a village of only one and a half square miles located in the town of Rockingham in Windham County. Bellows Falls historically was home to the first paper mill in Windham County and, later, a textile mill. Two railroads passed through Bellows Falls, contributing to its growth and prosperity as a mill town. Today, Victorian architecture is still apparent throughout the historic town that's home to the Green Mountain Railroad, operating seasonal scenic train excursions in the area, and the Adams Gristmill Warehouse. Today, Amtrak passes through Bellows Falls between St. Albans, Vermont, and Washington, D.C. Bellows Falls boasts a variety of listings in the National Register of Historic Places, including the Adams Gristmill Warehouse, the Bellows Falls Times Building, the Halls Covered Bridge and quite a few other buildings, chapels and other sites—including the Miss Bellows Fall Diner.

THE HISTORY OF THE MISS BELLOWS FALLS DINER

Located on Rockingham Street off Route 5 in Bellows Falls, Miss Bellows Falls Diner is a thirty-seat Worcester Lunch Car Company Car (#771) from 1941, manufactured in Worcester, Massachusetts. Originally, it was known as Frankie & Johnnie's Diner in Lowell, Massachusetts. It was built for John Korsak and Frank Willie in Lowell. When both men were called into military service for World War II, the diner was sold and trucked on a flatbed car of a train to Bellows Falls, where it replaced another diner at the same location. The original owner of the Miss Bellows Falls in Bellows Falls was Frank Cutler. The Miss Bellows Falls Diner has much of the original interior intact, with nine seats at the counter and five oak booths lining the outer wall. The Worcester Lunch Car Company became known for its porcelain and wood booths, along with patterned tile floors, marble counters and abundant stainless steel throughout the interior and exterior.

To preserve the history of the Miss Bellows Falls Diner, it was placed in the National Register of Historic Places in 1983, submitted by the owners at the time, Joanne Bush and Delmer "Dell" Bush. The Bushes were able to purchase the land the diner sits on, which had been leased since 1916. By the owners purchasing the land, the diner gained stronger roots in the community. The owners then chose to invest in preserving the structure and interior of the classic dining car once the land was owned. Following is an excerpt from the Bushes' National Register of Historic Places nomination with extensive details on the Miss Bellows Falls Diner and the premanufactured structure:

> *National Register Nomination Information:*
>
> *Statement of Significance:*
>
> *The "Miss Bellows Falls" Diner constitutes the only completely intact example in Vermont of the barrel-roofed Worcester Diner produced by the Worcester Lunch Car Company, a leading manufacturer during the first half of the twentieth century. The production date of the Miss Bellows Falls has not been established more definitely than being some years prior to 1942. Notwithstanding the fifty-year criterion of eligibility, the diner merits entry in the National Register for being a unique representative of early twentieth century roadside architecture, an importance enhanced by its continuously active use.*
>
> *Although probably not yet fifty years of age, the Miss Bellows Falls deserves the recognition of being entered in the National Register. The diner*

Above: The neon sign attracts visitors and locals alike at the Birdseye Diner in Castleton.

Right: Mugs at Vermont diners are as unique as the ambiance; this yellow mug adds a bright pop of color to the Birdseye's décor.

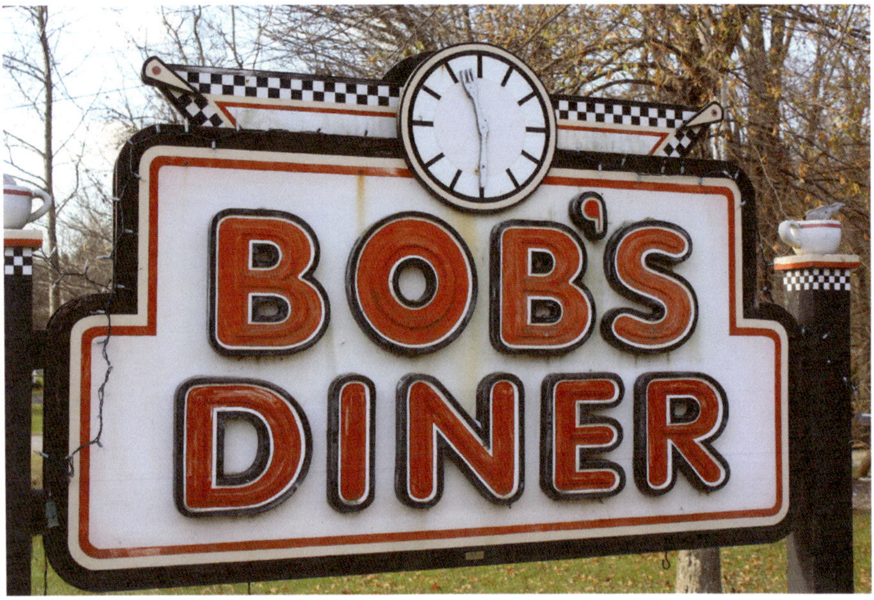

Above: From Route 11, Bob's Diner is a welcoming sight on the outskirts of Manchester.

Left: A favorite at Bob's Diner is the Smoked Salmon Eggs Benedict with house-made hollandaise.

The Blue Benn is a Silk City diner from 1948 with some of its original structure obstructed by blue awnings on the exterior.

The Chelsea Royal Diner's sign attracts passersby with its unique design and bright neon colors.

"Famous for Fine Food," the Chelsea Royal is a 1939 Worcester dining car.

The barrel-roofed diner touts booth service, available in the original dining car inside the Chelsea Royal Diner.

Above: The Chelsea Royal's bright-colored menu matches the sign outside and warmth of the waitstaff within.

Left: Cinnamon buns with copious icing are just one of the well-loved desserts at the Chelsea Royal.

Above: Miss Bellows Falls is a thirty-seat Worcester Lunch Car Company diner on Rockingham Street in Bellows Falls.

Left: The interior of the 1944 Silk City dining car remains in excellent condition.

Right: Maple Walnut Pie and bottomless coffee are always a good idea at the Country Girl Diner.

Below: The Windsor Diner features an all-you-can-eat fish fry.

The Springfield Royal Diner was operated as the Royal Diner in Kingston, New York, for forty-five years.

The Miss Lyndonville Diner is a staple of the community in Lyndonville, Vermont.

Right: The Miss Lyndonville Diner mugs boasts, "A really great place for enthusiastic diners of all ages," as quoted by *Yankee Magazine*.

Below: Hand-cut fries and a patty melt make for a delicious lunch at the Miss Lyndonville.

The rustic neon sign of the Parkway signals diner-goers of simpler times.

The owner of the Parkway Diner, Corey Gottfried (*center*), appears with two line cooks.

Left: The corned beef hash is a well-loved breakfast dish at the Parkway Diner.

Below: The Parkway Diner seats forty-nine customers behind its cherry-red façade.

The sign and logo for the Country Girl Diner feature a young girl with pigtails.

Left: Teal, cream and black tiles accent the interior of the Birdseye Diner with ample counter space.
Right: The colorful menu at the Birdseye Diner showcases the wide range of offerings, including a favorite, the Egg Cream Shake from the malt shop.

Left: Fluffy pancakes with Vermont maple syrup are a must at Henry's Diner.

Below: On weekends, Henry's Diner has a line down the block with customers waiting to get inside.

The yellow counter stools and booths at Henry's Diner add a bright pop of color to the historic diner.

Left: The modern interior of Henry's Diner has an open kitchen where those seated at the counter can observe the cooking.

Below: The Miss Bellows Falls features a barrel roof and many original details throughout the interior.

Left: A classic BLT and cup of coffee at the Chelsea Royal Diner with pickles made from cucumbers from the diner's own garden.

Below: The Parkway Diner is a classic Vermont diner located around the corner from the Burlington International Airport.

holds the exceptional importance of ranking among a dwindling number of pre-streamlined diners that preserve their original appearance and remain in active use. The Miss Bellows Falls represents a genre and period of American roadside architecture that has been bypassed both physically and culturally during the last two decades. Indeed, within Vermont's roadside environment, the Miss Bellows Falls has become singular survivor of an architectural and cultural expression now verging on extinction.

Ownership of the Miss Bellows Falls Diner has changed many times during its long history in Vermont, but the establishment has remained a central community gathering place for decades. Charlie Jarras owned the diner from 1990 to 2003, and before him, it was owned by Nelson Colborn. Jarras moved from Worcester to Bellows Falls and had been a patron of the diner before he purchased it. Since 2012, the diner has been owned by Brian McAllister, who also owns Father's Restaurant on Route 5, south of Bellows Falls. McAllister reopened the diner after it had been closed for a bit and wasn't serving the local community.

The Ambiance at the Miss Bellows Falls Diner

The Miss Bellows Falls is quite literally *on* Rockingham Street, with just a sidewalk separating the diner from the road. On the outside, large red letters on a gray background emphasize the name of the diner along with the words "Booth Service" on both sides. The rest of the diner is composed of enameled metal panels aside from the curved roof that has been covered with shingles. The Miss Bellows Falls Diner is one of few authentic barrel-roofed metal structure diners that remain. Inside, the original red marble counter, checkerboard tile floor, Formica tabletops and oak booths are accented by chrome details. The red stools complement the white-and-black tiled floor and the tabletops lined with red-and-white checkered tablecloths and curtains adorning the diner's windows, adding to the classic charm of the space. Above the counter, signs advertise "Hot Platters" and "Desserts," including banana splits, sundaes, ice cream and pies. On the counter, a decorative artistic flourish in red ties together the classic diner aesthetic. Very little on the interior has changed over time. Observe the original coolers still functioning behind the counter. The tables, booths, countertops and stools are all original as well, and some show their age. The exterior design is intact, and the diner spans sixteen feet wide and thirty feet long. The south door has a builder's plate affixed to it reading, "Worcester Diners #771, Worcester, Mass," proudly marking the history of this special roadside eatery in history and for Bellows Falls to all passersby.

FOOD AND BEVERAGE AT THE MISS BELLOWS FALLS DINER

The food at the Miss Bellows Falls Diner is some of the most classic of any Vermont diner and some of the best-priced home-cooked meals as well. Bottomless coffee is served from a quintessential diner mug—white with a sketch of the diner displayed on the front, along with the name of the diner and a mention of the diner's inclusion in the National Register. Breakfast is served all day, and lunch begins at 11:00 a.m. and runs until 2:00 p.m. For breakfast, choose from assorted muffins for $2.25 each or a more filling meal, such as Sausage Gravy with Biscuits or Buttermilk Pancakes with Chocolate Chips or Blueberries. Corned Beef Hash is available as a side for $3.25. For lunch, locals tend to enjoy the Hot Dog for $2.50 or a BLT, Grilled Cheese (offered with ham or tomato), sliced Ham and Cheese Sandwich, Tuna Melt, Fishwich or Fried Chicken Burger. In typical diner style, the menu also boasts a grilled Burger, weighing in at a third of a pound, along with a Classic Patty Melt, served with cooked onions on grilled rye bread with Swiss cheese. For heartier meals on the entrée menu, popular dishes include the Shepherd's Pie, Hot Open-Faced Turkey or Roast Beef with Gravy and American Chop Suey. The Miss Bellows Falls Diner also offers a variety of seafood, including Fried Clam Strips, a Fried Haddock Dinner, a Shrimp Basket and a Fried Seafood Basket.

Chapter 8

BOB'S DINER

(802) 362-4681
1130 Depot Street #2279
Manchester Center, Vermont 05255

AN INTRODUCTION TO MANCHESTER AND BOB'S DINER

Manchester is a shire town first settled in Bennington County in southern Vermont in 1764 and is situated between the Taconic Mountains to the west and the Green Mountains to the east. Manchester was historically known for its lumber companies, marble quarries and iron mines. Tourists started coming to the southern Vermont town with the onset of the railroad. Today, the town attracts many tourists from Connecticut, Massachusetts and New York for its culture, rich history and outdoor activities, along with the Manchester Designer Outlets, the well-known Equinox Resort, other boutique hotels and quaint Vermont inns and ample skiing in the area. Manchester is also home to Hildene, the Lincoln Family Home, and the Southern Vermont Arts Center for tourists interested in a visit rooted in the arts and history. Manchester is also a playground for outdoor recreation, as it's home to the American Museum of Fly Fishing and Orvis, along with the Land Rover Driving Experience School at the Equinox. The Northshire Bookstore is another attraction for the Manchester community. The historic

Bob's Diner is a Silk City replica of a '50s diner.

bookshop has played a role locally since 1976. Like at many diners, the bookstore has employees who have been working at the iconic shop for fifteen to twenty-five years, reveling in the role the bookstore has played in the lives of so many over the years. Located in Manchester Center off Route 11 on the outskirts of town, Bob's Diner is a Silk City replica of a '50s diner. Although the building itself isn't classic, the vintage vibe, warmth of the waitstaff, traditional diner fare and the role it plays in the community combine to replicate the essence of a classic diner.

The Ambiance at Bob's Diner

On Route 11/30 driving out of Manchester, Bob Diner's black, white and red sign with a clock in the center—iconic of classic diners—grabs drivers' attention. From the street, the shiny metal façade of Bob's Diner draws guests in. The black-and-white checkered tile on the exterior immediately creates a nostalgic Americana and Art Deco vibe. A clock matching the clock on the street at the sign marks the entrance to the space. Inside, diner guests might

Ample counter space and booths at Bob's give diner-goers even more opportunity to enjoy Bob Herbert's home cooking.

be fooled into thinking that this is a traditional dining car, as the replicated interior matches the classic diner aesthetic quite closely. Wooden booths with black leather cushions line the length of the diner, along with ample counter seating and a larger area for tables at one end of the elongated space. The black-and-white tiled floor is accented by red on the walls. A large, colorful jukebox matching the diner's décor sits at one end of the diner, available for requested tunes. As in many classic diners, the cooktop and griddle face out to the patrons.

Owner Bob Herbert can be seen behind the line flipping burgers, seasoning home fries and chatting with guests, many of whom he knows by name. Pet names are free flowing from chatty waitresses. "More coffee over there, Sweetness and Light?" "Have a nice day, Sir Honey!" "Here you go, Sugar Love!" "You just let me know, Sugar Doll, if I can get you a coffee to go, okay?" This particular waitress works the room, pouring refills of coffee without being asked, advising patrons of her favorite meals from the extensive menu, cracking jokes with regulars and telling others to bundle up and stay warm in the Vermont cold outside. She is what makes the diner a classic roadside eatery. In her presence, you immediately feel taken care of and nurtured.

FOOD AND BEVERAGE AT BOB'S DINER

The food at Bob's Diner is classic diner fare with ample breakfast options, hearty comfort food and juicy burgers at wallet-friendly prices. On the breakfast menu, the Skillets are some of the most popular options, including the Farmer Green Skillet (two eggs over spinach, mushroom, onions, tomatoes and home fries topped with Vermont cheddar), the Farmer Bob's Skillet (two eggs over bacon, sausage and home fries with Vermont cheddar) and the Cowboy Skillet (two eggs over ham, onions, green peppers and home fries with Vermont cheddar). The few twists the diner offers on a traditional Eggs Benedict are also big hits, including Eggs Sardau (two poached eggs on top of creamed spinach topped with homemade hollandaise), Eggs Blackstone (two poached eggs with bacon, sliced tomato with hollandaise on an English muffin) and Eggs Norway (two poached eggs with smoked salmon topped with dill hollandaise). For a sweet breakfast, Pancakes are hits in a variety of flavors, including Blueberry, Chocolate Chip, Mixed Berry, Banana Walnut, Apple Cinnamon Oatmeal and original Buttermilk, along with Texas Toast French Toast, Cinnamon Raisin French Toast, cornflake-crusted Eastern Mountain French Toast, Kahlua French Toast and French Toast stuffed with cream cheese and topped with berries.

On the lunch and dinner menu, classic diner favorites include a Monte Cristo, Hot Pastrami Sandwich, French Dip, California Club, Hot Dog, Grilled Reuben and Hot Open-Faced Sandwich, among others. Fried seafood is available, including a Clam Roll and Shrimp Platter, as well as a variety of burgers with classic ingredients and more inventive pairings. For a rugged, stick-to-your-ribs meal, Bob's Diner offers Beef or Chicken

Stroganoff, Turkey Dinner, American Goulash, Homemade Meatloaf and even a few Italian pasta dishes. Desserts at Bob's are ample, with homemade Rice Pudding, Fruit Pies, Cream Pies, Pecan Pies, Hot Fudge Sundaes, Belgian Waffle Sundaes and Banana "Splitilicious": a banana, three scoops of ice cream, hot fudge and whipped cream.

Bob's Diner is one of few in Vermont now serving a wide range of craft beers, which have become part and parcel of the Vermont brand and tourism for the Green Mountain State. Beers from Switchback Brewing, Fiddlehead Brewing, Long Trail Brewing and even local hard cider maker Citizen Cider and other local breweries are available in flights for guests who want to try all the beers on tap. The diner also sells wine and bottled beer, domestic and international. The diner is open at 6:30 a.m. every day and closes at 2:30 p.m. on Monday, Tuesday and Sunday and stays open for dinner until 8:30 p.m. on the other days of the week.

The Role of Bob's Diner in the Local Manchester Community

At Bob's Diner, the booths and counter are nearly always full of regulars and tourists who learn about the out-of-town eatery from locals as a must-visit in town for a quintessential small-town Vermont experience. Often on the weekends, there is a wait to dine at the popular roadside eatery. Price Padgett, who grew up in upstate New York just two miles from the Vermont border and has called New York City home for the past ten years, gushed about the overall experience at Bob's Diner. He shared, "Bob's is a special place to me. I bring a lot of friends up from the city, and it's always our go-to for a big breakfast to kick-start the day." Padgett went on, "They do a really good job of sourcing healthy, high-quality food, and the service is great. It's very old school. It feels like you're back in 1950 in there. Coffee refills, the whole thing."

Padgett remarked about the food, "They make these breakfasts in kettles that are particularly good—just a pile of veggies and eggs and breakfast meats. And it's definitely the kind of place that spans generations. It's fun to be in a place that caters to both twenty-five-year-olds and seventy-five-year-olds. It's not uncommon to get looped into another table's conversation, as it's not a big place; everyone is within earshot of the others. It hasn't changed a bit since I first went there fifteen years ago, which is part of what I love about Bob's."

Chapter 9

SPRINGFIELD ROYAL DINER

(802) 591-4374
363 River Street (Route 106)
Springfield, Vermont 05156
springfieldroyaldiner.com

AN INTRODUCTION TO SPRINGFIELD AND THE SPRINGFIELD DINER

Springfield, Vermont, is a town in southeastern Vermont covering nearly fifty square miles along the Black and Connecticut Rivers in Windsor County. Bordering New Hampshire, the town has a population of nearly nine thousand. In the late nineteenth century, the town became known as a center of manufacturing, and it is still regarded as an industrial town. In 1869, much of the town was washed away in a flood, and in 1880, a fire destroyed a large portion of Springfield as well. Several sites in Springfield are in the National Register of Historic Places, including the Eureka Schoolhouse, which is the oldest one-room schoolhouse in the state, along with the Hartness House and the Gould's Mill Bridge. Springfield was put on the national map in 2007 when the town was chosen to host the premiere of *The Simpsons Movie*, which was set in the town of Springfield, like in the television show. Today, Springfield is home to the Community College of Vermont and a University of Vermont campus.

The Springfield Royal Diner is a rare Mahony Diner car from 1957.

THE HISTORY OF THE SPRINGFIELD ROYAL DINER

The Springfield Royal Diner is a rare Mahony Diner Car from the mid-1950s, originally seating sixty people. The Jerry O'Mahoney Diner Company of Elizabeth, New Jersey, produced roughly two thousand diners from 1917 to 1952. Mahony Diners, Inc., lasted for only two years, from 1956 to 1958, in Kearney, New Jersey, and only built four diners, one of which is the Springfield Royal Diner today. The Springfield Royal Diner is thought to be the last Mahony diner built and the last remaining. It was previously known as the Royal Diner and was located in Kingston, New York. There, it operated for forty-five years until it went out of business in 2001. As the Royal Diner in Kingston, the diner was operated by Lee Konja and partner Angelo Papaleonardos. Konja worked behind the counter for forty years. First located at 516 Albany Avenue in Kingston, it later moved to Route 28. When Konja decided it was time to retire, the future of the diner was in danger. Luckily, the American Diner Museum, based in Providence, Rhode Island, stepped in and saved the historical diner from a likely demise.

At that point, the twenty-eight-ton diner was purchased and brought to Springfield in 2002. Matthew Alldredge and Laurentiu Traineau joined together to purchase the diner after layoffs and business closings in Springfield. The duo had been redeveloping businesses and prided themselves on adding to the Springfield economy—and so they did with the purchase of the Royal Diner, along with a third partner, Roger Vawvey. Together, the three formed the Springfield Diner Corporation and brought the Royal Diner from Route 28 in Ulster, New York, to Springfield, Vermont.

The diner was brought to Vermont by O.B. Hill Trucking and Rigging Company and had a police escort into the town of Springfield. Prior to being moved, the vestibule was removed and systems like heating, air conditioning and ventilation were disconnected. It's said that during the moving of the diner to Vermont in February 2002, a snowstorm hit, and the flatbed was stuck in Brattleboro, Vermont, for two days. The diner eventually made it on March 1, 2002, and has remained in its same location since then. Once in Vermont, the diner underwent significant cleanup and restoration, as well as additions to the right and left sides. The diner reopened with a groundbreaking ceremony in February 2003 and operated for a few years before an abrupt closing. During that time, Alldredge added onto the building to create the Precision Valley Corvette Museum to showcase his collection of cars. Since the diner's closing in August 2007, at which point Alldredge put the diner up for sale for $759,000, ownership has changed a number of times, along with the name. In 2008, the diner was leased by Alldredge to Silvestre "Sly" Gallegos, who also at the time owned the Golden Egg in Saxtons River, Vermont. At one point, it was called the Royal Diner and Pancake House. The diner briefly closed again in 2011 after two floods, at which point Nina Howe, a waitress at the diner, purchased it with the help of her family. Since then, it has reopened once again, striving to play a continuing role in the Springfield community.

THE AMBIANCE AT THE SPRINGFIELD ROYAL DINER

From Route 106, which winds through Springfield, the metal-clad diner looks impressive, situated against a wooded backdrop. The diner measures seventeen by forty-eight feet and seats roughly eighty guests. Inside, the original pink counters are intact, with ample stools and booths for sitting, along with original terrazzo floors. The kitchen is located in the back rather than behind the counter and has been upgraded to a commercial kitchen for efficiencies with preparing the food served within. Much of the interior is original, including the booths, tables, stools, counter and back-counter space. The original pink and chrome interior remains, along with pink vinyl booths and Formica counters. The Springfield Royal Diner is the only classic diner in Vermont to boast a pale pink interior and includes the most metal on the façade of any diner in the state.

FOOD AND BEVERAGE AT THE SPRINGFIELD ROYAL DINER

The Springfield Royal Diner's tagline is "Eat, Treat and Live '50's style." Food at the Springfield Royal Diner is largely traditional and inexpensive, consisting of a Grilled Ham and Cheese sandwich; BLT; Turkey Club; Reuben; Meatloaf Melt; Monte Cristo sandwich; and wraps, including a Grilled Veggie Wrap, Chicken Caesar Wrap and Crispy Chicken Wrap. The menu also includes two unique burgers in addition to its classic burger: a Rodeo Burger with cheddar, onion rings and barbecue sauce and a Five-Alarm Burger with spicy pepper jack cheese and jalapeños. For breakfast, the diner has fun with inventive takes on classic diner food, like Cinnamon Roll Pancakes and Salted Caramel Banana Pancakes. For dessert, the diner offers unique cupcakes, including Raspberry Champagne and Root Beer Float. The diner is open daily from 6:00 a.m. to 4:00 p.m., with take-out available.

Chapter 10

WINDSOR DINER

(802) 674-5555
135 Main Street
Windsor, Vermont 05089
Facebook.com/1952vt

AN INTRODUCTION TO WINDSOR AND THE WINDSOR DINER

Windsor, Vermont, is a quaint, historic downtown in Windsor County in southeastern Vermont, home to roughly 3,750 residents. Windsor is the birthplace of Vermont, where the constitution of Vermont was adopted in 1777, although Vermont didn't become a state until 1791. In the mid-nineteenth century, Windsor became known as a center of innovation for the high-tech mechanical work being done in the town. Today, Windsor boasts a self-guided walking tour of more than forty historic buildings, including the Windsor Public Library, Saint-Gaudens National Historical Site, Windsor House and the Constitution House. Windsor's Artisan Park is home to Simon Pearce—the popular Vermont glassblower and potter—along with a craft brewery, distillery, cheese shop and sculpture garden. In addition to its rich history, Windsor is also a popular destination in Vermont for mountain biking and hiking in Mount Ascutney State Park, along with kayaking and tubing on the Connecticut River.

THE HISTORY OF THE WINDSOR DINER

The Windsor Diner has played a role in the Windsor community since 1939. At that point, the diner was composed of two dining cars. The diner that currently touts the name the Windsor Diner located on Main Street in Windsor is a Worcester Lunch Company Car (#835) with construction dating to 1952. The diner was originally installed in Fitchburg, Massachusetts. The original curved roof is now hidden by a metal roof, and an extension to the side holds additional seats. The original orientation of the diner has been kept intact. Counter stools face the cooking area, while booths line the outside wall. A sign in the interior underscores the year it was built and the model number of the dining car. The diner's motto is "Good Food Fast" and is found on the northern wall above a neon-lit sign.

According to owner Theresa Taylor, "Our diner is a 1952 model and was built in Fitchburg, Massachusetts. In 1961, Chip Miller, who owned the 1939 diner in the same location, wanted to upgrade to a more modern version. He owned a construction company called Miller Construction and decided to move it to Windsor, which is the diner we now have. Its original name was Ray's Diner in Fitchburg and was in a town with several others. My family has owned the diner only since 2002, but our family roots go far back to this town of Windsor."

Taylor explained her connection to the diner and her history in the food service industry: "I started working in the restaurant business in 1989 as a teenager at the Pleasant Restaurant in Claremont, New Hampshire, a family-style restaurant. I then worked at several other restaurants in a similar style;

The old Windsor Diner, circa 1939, is depicted in a newspaper article. *Courtesy of Theresa Taylor.*

I've worked at many my first fifteen years. Family-style restaurants seem to come and go in our area due to very high taxes. I resolved to try cooking in a nursing home. No creativity was allowed. Next, I tried Walmart bakery and loved that, but after two years, my wrist started to develop carpal tunnel, and I ended my employment there. I decided at this time to open my own bakery and was hoping with less repeated work and a variety of items it would make a go for me and Claremont. Unfortunately, it was short-lived, and we closed it after only two years."

Taylor went on, "The next stop for me was then known as Dan's Windsor Diner. My dad, Fred Borcuk, purchased it, with the arrangement that we would run it together. After about six years, I was ready to purchase the diner with my husband, Mark Taylor. I'm now in my sixteenth year, and it's the most rewarding thing I've ever done. Our original Worcester Lunch Car draws a good crowd seasonally and regulars and skiers in the colder months. Our original lunch car is in great shape, mostly due to the fact that it was made almost last in production out of these style cars. This has helped it survive longer and in better condition. It's truly a rare find."

THE AMBIANCE AT THE WINDSOR DINER

Located a few steps from the road on Main Street, the Windsor Diner has a prominent, hard-to-miss location. The exterior is red metal with a red roof. An "All You Can Eat Fish Fry" sign—every Thursday night from 5:00 p.m. to 8:00 p.m. for $10.95, including haddock, fries and slaw—sits in the window. Stainless steel accentuates the windows and positions the diner as vintage. Red-and-white striped flower boxes sit under the windows. An open sign flies freely next to the sign for the Windsor Diner, topped with a classic "Enjoy Coca-Cola" sign. Inside, the eye is drawn to large neon signs at the end of the counter. One sign reads, "Good Fast Food. Welcome to the Windsor Diner. Worcester Lunch Car Company," and the other reads, "Best Hot Dogs in Vermont. Delicious hand-packed ice cream. Shakes. Cones. Sundaes." The red exterior carries inside with red-and-yellow tile work at the counter, with red and stainless-steel counter stools and intricately tiled floors. Behind the counter, you'll see the original cooler in yellow, along with a stainless cooktop, coffee station and glass containers for storage. Above the counter are announcements, including Daily Specials, such as Stuffed Pork Chops, Lasagna with salad, a Petite or King-Sized Prime Rib Au Jus, BBQ Beef Brisket and daily menu items on another centered announcement board, along with information on the history of the Worcester dining car. Along the windows, wooden booths with red padding add to the homey atmosphere.

FOOD AND BEVERAGE AT THE WINDSOR DINER

Along with the blueprint and cost sheet for the construction of the Windsor Diner dating back to 1952, Taylor provided a snapshot of the diner's menus on Friday, November 24, 1961, and Saturday, November 25, 1961. Macaroni Tomato Soup was $0.15 for a cup or $0.25 for a bowl. A choice of juice was $0.15. The extensive menu of hearty meals ranged from Pot Roast of Beef for $0.99 to Baked Beans for $0.50, with the addition of franks for $0.75. Fresh Oyster Stew was available for $0.85, and Grilled Veal Cutlets or a Grilled Ham Steak were $0.95 each. Even then, the menu had ample seafood offerings, from Fried Deep Sea Scallops for $0.99 to Fried Shrimp. Sides were a choice of potato—mashed or French fried—or vegetable with coleslaw, beets or succotash. Homemade pies were also a draw in a variety of flavors for $0.20 for a slice for $0.30 for a la mode. Strawberry-rhubarb pie, blueberry pie, raisin pie, lemon pie, date pie, apple pie, custard chocolate pie, banana pie and coconut cream pie, along with pineapple cream pudding and bread pudding, rounded out the dessert offerings.

According to Taylor, current diner favorites include daily specials like Meatloaf, Mac and Cheese and Liver and Onions. "We run special omelets daily like meat lover's or veggie and cheese. I have created my own bread and pancake mix recipes over time, and they seem to be consistent to our customers' liking," Taylor said. "Our most unique dish at the diner is our homemade hash. It's our own recipe and takes two days to make. It has lots of steps and is made in bulk size. It freezes well, so we choose to make a bigger batch to save time in the long run," she shared. "We make a corned beef dinner to start off. Then we shred all of the ingredients and combine and place it on large sheets. We add the corned beef juice back in and some beef stock and black pepper and bake it off for about half hour. This is a great fresh flavor of comfort food."

"We like to keep our food similar to what you would expect at a local diner. We do offer many salads and other items to accommodate the needs of special diets like gluten-free and sugar-free diets," Taylor explained.

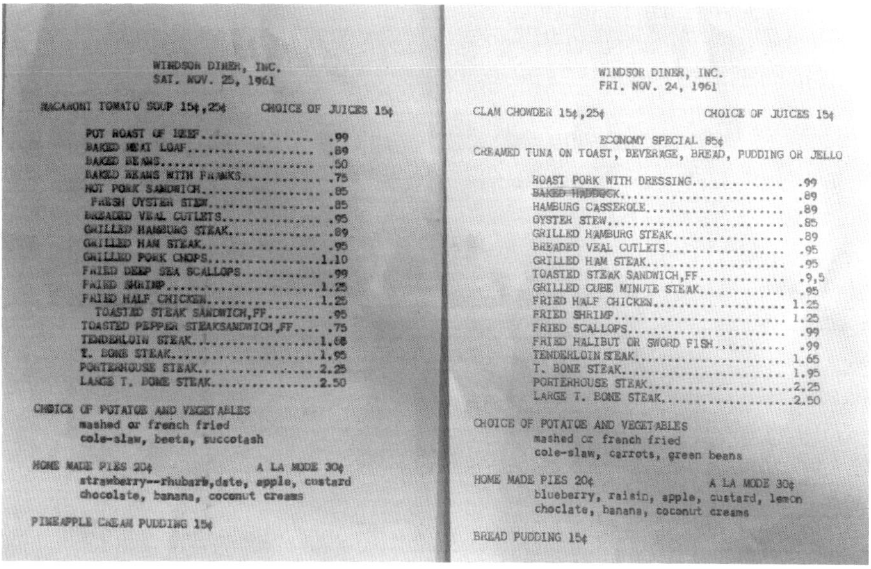

WINDSOR DINER, INC.
SAT. NOV. 25, 1961

MACARONI TOMATO SOUP 15¢,25¢ CHOICE OF JUICES 15¢

POT ROAST OF BEEF.................. .99
BAKED MEAT LOAF.................... .89
BAKED BEANS........................ .50
BAKED BEANS WITH FRANKS............ .75
HOT PORK SANDWICH.................. .85
FRESH OYSTER STEW.................. .85
BREADED VEAL CUTLETS............... .95
GRILLED HAMBURG STEAK.............. .89
GRILLED HAM STEAK.................. .95
GRILLED PORK CHOPS.................1.10
FRIED DEEP SEA SCALLOPS............ .99
FRIED SHRIMP.......................1.25
FRIED HALF CHICKEN.................1.25
TOASTED STEAK SANDWICH,FF.......... .95
TOASTED PEPPER STEAKSANDWICH,FF.... .75
TENDERLOIN STEAK...................1.68
T. BONE STEAK......................1.95
PORTERHOUSE STEAK..................2.25
LARGE T. BONE STEAK................2.50

CHOICE OF POTATOE AND VEGETABLES
mashed or french fried
cole-slaw, beets, succotash

HOME MADE PIES 20¢ A LA MODE 30¢
strawberry--rhubarb,date, apple, custard
chocolate, banana, coconut creams

PINEAPPLE CREAM PUDDING 15¢

WINDSOR DINER, INC.
FRI. NOV. 24, 1961

CLAM CHOWDER 15¢,25¢ CHOICE OF JUICES 15¢

ECONOMY SPECIAL 85¢
CREAMED TUNA ON TOAST, BEVERAGE, BREAD, PUDDING OR JELLO

ROAST PORK WITH DRESSING.............. .99
~~BAKED HADDOCK~~.......................... .89
HAMBURG CASSEROLE..................... .89
OYSTER STEW........................... .85
GRILLED HAMBURG STEAK................. .89
BREADED VEAL CUTLETS.................. .95
GRILLED HAM STEAK..................... .95
TOASTED STEAK SANDWICH,FF............. .9,5
GRILLED CUBE MINUTE STEAK............. .95
FRIED HALF CHICKEN.................... 1.25
FRIED SHRIMP.......................... 1.25
FRIED SCALLOPS........................ .99
FRIED HALIBUT OR SWORD FISH........... .99
TENDERLOIN STEAK...................... 1.65
T. BONE STEAK......................... 1.95
PORTERHOUSE STEAK.....................2.25
LARGE T. BONE STEAK...................2.50

CHOICE OF POTATOE AND VEGETABLES
mashed or french fried
cole-slaw, carrots, green beans

HOME MADE PIES 20¢ A LA MODE 30¢
blueberry, raisin, apple, custard, lemon
choclate, banana, coconut creams

BREAD PUDDING 15¢

This original Windsor Diner menu from November 1961 shows the variety of meals available at affordable prices. *Courtesy of Theresa Taylor.*

"Tripe and liver and onions are also on the favorite daily menu, and yes, we sell lots."

Homemade desserts at the Windsor Diner are a draw, from apple pie, blackberry pie, lemon meringue pie and pumpkin pie to coconut cake, strawberry shortcake, maple bread pudding and fried dough. Served up with the diner's Colombian coffee, these desserts—along with homemade muffins and doughnuts—are a perfect sweet treat to end a meal. The Windsor Diner is one of a handful of Vermont diners that serves dinner along with breakfast and lunch. Like many diners, the Windsor Diner is a cash-only restaurant, with an ATM inside.

THE ROLE OF THE WINDSOR DINER IN THE LOCAL COMMUNITY

One of the fundamental tasks of any diner is to play a role in the community it serves, for locals and travelers alike. The Windsor Diner does more than just serve guests. It is an active community member, hosting fundraisers and events to celebrate those in the community doing good work. Taylor commented, "In our community, we serve three meals a day. We donate meals to our local events like rotary clubs, school fundraisers and state trooper events. We have also been known to run drawings to support the local Lucy Mackenzie [Humane Society] in West Windsor. We provide a place to meet for families and small groups up to thirty. Since the diner has been here, it's been known as a gathering place for family time, reunions and meetings of all kinds."

Locals aren't the only ones who are drawn to the Windsor Diner. It's a popular eatery for skiers in the area and travelers driving through town. Haylee Schmidt, who lives in Connecticut, shared her experience at the Windsor Diner: "I've been to the Windsor Diner a few times when my family has visited Vermont for skip trips or getaways....The waitress helped us find tables to seat our large group and made us feel right at home with her quick wit and welcoming smile. We all hurriedly ordered breakfast food, and I got my personal favorite: chocolate chip pancakes. It was about eight o'clock at night, we had all just come back from a long day of skiing. All of us were exhausted, while half of us were grumpy. And mind you, Windsor, Vermont, isn't exactly known for its plethora of restaurants and places to eat. Still, the

The Windsor Diner is a Worcester Lunch Car (#835) dating to 1952.

friendly service, comfortable ambiance and delicious food had us all cheerful and laughing together in no time. One of my favorite memories from our Vermont trip was sitting in that enchanting Windsor Diner, laughing with my friends and family."

Kristina Danahy, originally from Arlington, Virginia, who now lives in Boston, said, "The dining car setting and local flair make the Windsor Diner unique. We felt like we were going back in time! We went in for a late brunch, so it was pretty calm when we got in. The staff was so nice to us and were gracious even when my toddler got biscuit crumbs everywhere. Corned beef hash, coffee and pancakes are a must. Diners are a great place to enjoy comfort food, local flavor conversations with your loved ones and people watching."

Larry Swift, from Claremont, New Hampshire, remembers his trip to the Windsor Diner fondly. "We visited on a cold Saturday night, and there were not a lot of customers—maybe half a dozen, not including my seven-year-old son and I," Swift shared. "I didn't see much of a kids' menu, but the waitress who was taking our order was nice enough to recommend that my son get a half order of chicken fingers. I ordered a bacon cheeseburger with fries, and neither one of us left hungry; the helpings were generous. The diner is smack-dab in the middle of the town, so it's more of a meeting place for the locals. It's like Cheers; everyone knows everybody, and the waitstaff knows what the regulars order every time they come in. Places like the Windsor Diner are great because years ago, that's where everyone went, whether it was a quick bite while passing through town or catching up on the local town gossip. I like diners because they don't change. It's like a window to the past. I like watching the meals get made on the flattop right in front of you, the swiveling stools, the stainless trim, the plain white coffee cups." At the Windsor Diner, it's about the complete experience—the comforting meals, companionship and memory making.

Chapter 11

THE BIRDSEYE DINER

(802) 468-5817
590 Main Street
Castleton, Vermont 05735
birdseyediner.com

AN INTRODUCTION TO CASTLETON AND THE BIRDSEYE DINER

Castleton, Vermont, is a college town of approximately four thousand residents bordering New York on the western part of the state, located in Rutland County. The town is five miles east of the New York/Vermont border and fifteen miles west of Rutland. Originally primarily an agricultural community, Castleton grew to develop as a leader in the slate and marble industries in Vermont. Once the railroad came to town in 1854, the town of Castleton began to become a tourist destination due to its proximity to Lake Bomoseen, a freshwater lake between Castleton and Hubbardton. Castleton University is located in the small Vermont town and was founded in 1787. The university is a big draw for the town, as it offers some of the most diverse curricula out of any universities in the state. One of Castleton's most well-known landmarks is Birdseye Mountain, named after Amos Bird, who was one of the town's first settlers, and after whom the Birdseye Diner is also named. Interestingly, today Birdseye Mountain is a retired ski mountain.

The Birdseye is a gathering place for coffee and conversation in downtown Castleton.

It originally opened in 1962 with a rope tow to serve nearby Castleton University students and students from Green Mountain College in Poultney. It closed in the late 1960s after years of poor snow conditions. Although others tried to reopen it and find different usages for the land, including the installation of a swimming pool and a camping base area and the idea for a summertime Vermont theme park on the property, the mountain never took off again. Today, Castleton is a quaint college town known for its bicycling and walking trails, being part of the Stone Valley Scenic Byway and nearby Crystal Beach for outdoor activities.

THE HISTORY OF THE BIRDSEYE DINER

The Birdseye Diner, sitting on Main Street in downtown Castleton, is a Silk City dining car from 1946, manufactured in Paterson, New Jersey. The name Birdseye is a reference to Mount Birdseye or Birdseye Mountain. The chrome dining car was delivered to Castleton via tractor trailer to replace the former wooden Birdseye Diner, which had burned down in 1960. Prior to that, the dining car had been in service for eighteen years and then returned to the "factory for a face lift," according to the history as told by the Birdseye Diner's website. Over the years, the diner has been called the Campus Diner, Jim's and T.J.'s and has undergone extensive modifications, including an extended kitchen and new façade.

The current owners, Pam and John Rehlen, have owned the diner since November 1995, when the Paterson Vehicle Company dining car underwent significant renovations, in essence restoring it to its original condition. Most of the interior chrome was removed under the watch of Daniel Zilka, a professional diner restorer, in order to restore the dining car to the way it would have looked in the 1940s. In 1996, the Rehlens removed a pitched roof and barn-board siding to include a curved roof like the diner would have had in the '40s. In 1997, they added on a dining room, which allowed for an additional forty seats. In 1998, the diner added outdoor seating for warmer weather. Before the renovations in 1997, the interior featured the same blue-and-yellow checkered tiles on the counter and brown booths lining the length of the dining car. Over time, the shingled roof was stripped off and a new metal roof was added with a dramatic neon sign, helping the building to pop in downtown Castleton.

THE AMBIANCE AT THE BIRDSEYE DINER

The Birdseye has some of the best curb appeal of any diner in Vermont, with its neon sign sitting majestically atop the chrome dining car. In the summer months, red umbrellas and outdoor seating invite guests to dine outside. Inside, there are lovingly worn red booths with aqua, black and cream diamond-patterned tile work and seafoam counters. A Birdseye clock in bright blue sits in the middle of the diner, which has room for twenty at the bar and booths lining the dining car with full windows adding natural light to the space. "Love Potion No. 9" plays in the background, and local construction workers and college students alike enjoy $2.99 breakfasts, a special during the week. Behind the bar, you can find framed original advertising for the Silk City diner, including mention of "an all-cash business with all cash profits" that a purchaser could have both of. "Big Profits, Modern investment, with America's finest diner" finishes out the ad.

FOOD AND BEVERAGE AT THE BIRDSEYE DINER

The Birdseye Diner is one of few in Vermont that serves three square meals a day, offering breakfast starting at 7:00 a.m. through a late-night dinner at 9:00 p.m., satisfying the nearby college crowd. One of the huge draws for breakfast at the Birdseye Diner is the $2.99 breakfast, with a sign out front advertising the not-too-good-to-be-true deal. Cinnamon French toast dusted with powdered sugar and a side of bacon for $2.99? Add a coffee and locals can enjoy a hearty, homemade breakfast just like Mom used to make for close to $5.00. The menu contains traditional diner fare with few surprises. For breakfast, a New England favorite is Sausage Gravy and Biscuits or large Chocolate Chip Pancakes or Blueberry Pancakes, served with real Vermont maple syrup. Classic Eggs Benedict and Steak and Eggs are other local favorites for a filling meal to start off the day.

On the lunch and dinner menus, burgers abound. Choose from the Chili Burger (served with the diner's spicy chili), the Highland Burger (served with Canadian bacon, melted cheese and a spicy Dijon mustard sauce), the Bistro Burger (served with diced tomato, onions, garlic and basil) or the South of the Border Burger (served with spicy salsa and melted Monterey Jack cheese). Traditionally, all burgers are served with lettuce, tomato and hand-cut, crispy French fries. For the fries, the diner offers unique dipping sauces, including Gilroy Garlic and Craig's Honey Dijon. Sandwiches are classic diner fare: the Birdseye Club; Classic BLT; Turkey Sandwich; Tuna Melt; Hot Sandwich with turkey, roast beef, pork or meatloaf covered with homemade gravy; Hot Dog; Philly Cheese Steak; Grilled Reuben; and Fish Filet sandwich. For comfort food dinners, the Birdseye prides itself on dishes like Roasted Pork, Roasted Turkey and Roast Beef Dinner served with potatoes, vegetables and gravy; Sautéed Beef Liver with bacon and caramelized onions; the Birdseye Meatloaf, the house specialty; and a range of Italian comfort foods as well, including Lasagna, Stuffed Shells and Chicken Parmigiana.

It's never too early to indulge in dessert at the Birdseye Diner. A specials board for desserts advertises lime, raspberry and strawberry Jell-O; sundaes with Butterfingers and strawberry shortcake; slices of pie and slices of cake; and ample ice cream and pudding offerings. The Birdseye Diner also has its own malt shop for a quintessential diner drink. Egg Cream in chocolate or vanilla (no egg, no cream—just milk, syrup and seltzer), Malted Milkshakes and Root Beer Floats are a big hit with college students escaping the dining hall. The Birdseye also sells its own swag, including iconic yellow Birdseye mugs, along with Birdseye ball caps in black, khaki and navy. It also sells

A plate of French toast and bacon for $2.99 with a bottomless coffee is a hard deal to beat at the Birdseye.

pancake mix and blueberry pancake mix from Brown Family Farm, a local farm in the Castleton community, along with thirty-two-ounce jugs of Vermont maple syrup. Many of the products and ingredients used at the Birdseye Diner come from close by, including all milk products from Thomas Dairy of Rutland, eggs from Maple Meadow Farm and potatoes from Perry's Potatoes in Hampton, New York, just over the Vermont border. The menu proudly displays these partnerships, showcasing how sourcing close-to-home products is important for most local eateries in Vermont, even in the comfort food classics that diners offer.

THE ROLE OF THE BIRDSEYE DINER IN THE LOCAL COMMUNITY

For years, the Birdseye Diner has served Castleton locals and college students, along with Lake Bomoseen summer tourists. Middlebury resident Amey Ryan attended Castleton University (then Castleton State College) when there were only two places in town to eat: "A pizza joint and a diner. Both were owned by the same family, from what I was told. The diner was a classic. Sticky booth seats, pies and muffins on the counter, friendly 'lifers' behind the counter. It was basic, good grub. We would generally hit up the diner after a morning hike or hangover. In either case, I was never disappointed!"

Ryan continued, "One of the things I love about diners in general, and this is true of the Birdseye Diner as well, is that it's often a healthy mix of locals and/or regulars and those traveling through our state or attending the nearby college. This was true back then in Castleton, and it's true here in Middlebury, and it's true in Burlington. I love that! Since I was in school (1995–99), the diner has been expanded and updated. I've had a chance to go back on several reunion or homecoming weekends, and it is always the first choice of the group. It's a comfortable and welcoming place to be in Castleton."

Holly Leasan, born and raised in the neighboring town of Fair Haven, Vermont, said, "My first time at the Birdseye was when I was maybe fourteen for brunch with a cousin, and I've been going there since. It's one of those places where you go twice, and the people remember you. It's amazing for both college kids and families alike. Every time I head to the Birdseye, I see such a vast array of people, old and young, all enjoying their stay. I've had many conversations with people of different ages, races and reaches while sitting at their counter. I hope to continue doing so." Leasan went on to rave about the food too. "My favorite official item is their Eggs Benedict or one of their breakfast plates," she said. "But I really enjoy their curly fries with cheddar and gravy. A twist on poutine is a personal favorite of mine. The staff is phenomenal and hardworking but still open to great conversation. They genuinely care, and you can see that. I go back because it's hard to beat the staff and the food. You have to cherish that, and when the entire place is packed on a Saturday or Sunday morning, it's easy to tell people do just that."

Brett Doonan, who grew up in Westport, Connecticut, and currently lives in Los Angeles, has been going to the Birdseye Diner for years, he says. "Our family has been going to the Birdseye our entire lives," Doonan shared. "We took a trip to Europe when we were young and brought our Birdseye T-shirts and took a photo in front of the Eiffel Tower. They've had that photo in the diner right up front for almost ten years now. What makes the Birdseye Diner so unique are the incredible dishes, great staff, amazing owner and having a local Bomoseen eatery in the community. We love seeing familiar faces, and everyone we bring to Castleton always leaves the Birdseye with a mug, hat or T-shirt. The ambiance is something that you can't really compare to anywhere else. The old-fashioned diner style… the side room that has beautiful murals…and if you are sitting outside, the people watching is the best."

Chapter 12

THE DINER

(802) 388-2397
66 Merchants Row
Middlebury, Vermont 05753

Author's Note: Sadly, on June 1, 2018, the Diner was sold to its neighbor the Town Hall Theater on Merchants Row in Middlebury. Although the space remains intact for now, the building is no longer serving its original function as a gathering place for locals and college students alike. This diner sale is a strong reminder of the importance of supporting classic eateries to keep them afloat during the evolution of modern times. They all need our support and patronage to preserve the role they play in our local communities.

AN INTRODUCTION TO MIDDLEBURY AND THE DINER

Middlebury, Vermont, located in west-central Vermont, is the shire town, or county seat, of Addison County and is home to Middlebury College, the Henry Sheldon Museum of Vermont History, the Vermont Folk Life Center, the Town Hall Theater, the Pulp Mill Covered Bridge and the Halpin Covered Bridge. In the center of town, the Otter Creek River falls, creating a natural focal point in the quintessential Vermont college town. The town green, overlooked by the iconic Middlebury Inn, hosts craft fairs, chili cook-offs and music festivals. With roughly 8,500 full-time residents, the town population expands when Middlebury College is in session

The Diner in Middlebury, formerly known as Steve's Park Diner, is an eatery that previously brought college students, locals and tourists alike together.

and during the summers, when the college hosts its renowned Language Schools. The town of Middlebury is rich in history and culture. The downtown shopping area boasts galleries, a coffee shop, a nontraditional movie theater and independently owned clothing shops and gift boutiques. Middlebury is the kind of small Vermont town where everyone says hello in passing, and more often than not, a trip into town means running into a friend or acquaintance.

In the mid-1930s, Middlebury got its first diner. Businessman Jack Swanson, from Massachusetts, brought the metal diner to Middlebury by train bed and navigated the tight streets of downtown Middlebury, according to an article written in Middlebury's *Valley Voice* newspaper by Larry Johnson. The diner—complete with a metal frame and wooden wheels—made its way across Seymour Street and parked next to Butterfield's gas station on Main Street. At that time, the average meal cost about fifty cents. Coffee was five cents, or for a real steal, a cup of coffee and slice of pie could be purchased for fifteen cents together. The diner was originally named the Val-Do-Mar Diner. In the 1930s, the Val-Do-Mar advertised in the *Middlebury Campus*, Middlebury College's newspaper, unifying college students with the town. The advertisement in volume 33, issue 1, dating to October 1935, simply reads, "Val-Do-Mar Diner. It's Quality and Price Today, We Give the Best of Both." In an ad from volume 33, issue 25 from April 1936, the text reads, "Val-Do-Mar Diner. We are closing all accounts for this year. CREDIT CLOSES MAY 1. ALL BILLS PAYABLE ON OR BEFORE THAT DATE."

THE HISTORY OF THE DINER

Sometime in the early 1940s, the diner moved once again onto Merchants Row, next to the town hall (now the Town Hall Theater). At this point, the diner was purchased and sold a number of times. It shuffled between several owners until it was purchased by two brothers, Charlie and Francis Smith, in 1946 after the war. At this point, it was renamed the Park Diner. In 1951, the original building began to fall apart. Its metal structure was removed, and the diner was rebuilt in the location where it stands today. It was later called the Lemon Fair Restaurant, named after the slow-flowing Lemon Fair River just outside town. At that point, Middlebury's diner was owned by local Corrado Salini. Open for breakfast, lunch and dinner, the Lemon Fair Restaurant carved out its place and role as a locals' dining establishment in the Middlebury community. Then, in 1989, locals Steve and Beth Dow purchased the diner, changing its name to Steve's Park Diner. They focused solely on serving breakfast and lunch, omitting the dinner service. Steve had attended the Culinary Institute of America and had been working in Middlebury College's Dining Service for sixteen years before they took the plunge into owning an iconic Vermont diner.

With the Dows at the helm, the restaurant quickly became a fixture in downtown Middlebury with typical diner fare, embellished with maple syrup from the Dows' own sugarbush—a collection of maple syrup trees where sap is procured and boiled into sap. The Dows' maple syrup business was called Sugar Brook Maple Company and produced nearly seven hundred gallons of syrup, which was served at the diner for the authentic maple syrup experience.

In a community that strives to improve town-gown relations regularly, a tradition started in 1989 when the then owners of the diner advertised a 5:00 a.m. breakfast before commencement and served over two hundred breakfasts in the first year. The second year, the diner served over five hundred breakfasts. The tradition still continues, with the diner acting as the site of the final celebration of Middlebury College students' time on campus before commencement. Steve's Park Diner wasn't just a hit with the local college students, however. When the Dows owned the restaurant, the local football team from Middlebury Union High School would dine in for breakfast before games. For the last game of the season, breakfast would be donated by the Dows, which became tradition and a bit of superstition to ensure the high school football team won the last game of the season, fueled by good local fare.

In April 2014, the Dows passed ownership of Steve's Park Diner to a young West Addison couple, Caetlin Harwood and Carl Roesch, who had worked at restaurants around Vermont, including Basin Harbor Club in Addison, American Flatbread in downtown Middlebury and Tourterelle Restaurant and Inn in the neighboring town of New Haven. Some new paint—including brightening the exterior with a gray façade trimmed with subdued blue, painting it a warm golden yellow with creamy trim, accented by a new red sign and logo with a built-in clock to always keep passersby informed—freshened up and modernized the space. A new menu with more innovative diner fare showed the new owners were also willing to modernize the offerings of this classic Vermont diner, not just the curb appeal.

Interestingly, there was back and forth over whether the name Steve's Park Diner would remain in the purchase of the iconic Middlebury diner. Harwood and Roesch took to social media to find a new name for the community establishment, crowdsourcing the new name. They eventually settled on "The Diner, a Middlebury Classic." Since owning the diner, Harwood has come to truly understand the role the diner plays in the community. "The Diner serves a major role in bringing townspeople together," she explained. "It serves as a meeting place and a common location where folks can come together and share space without the distractions of everyday life. It allows people to share a part of their day with others, share a meal or a cup of coffee and be a part of something that has been an institution for generations. The diner has been a focal point and meeting place for over seventy years in Middlebury."

In fact, the Diner still employs several people who have been there for decades. Harwood shared, "We have many regulars who enjoy being on a first-name basis with the servers who have their meals memorized. These regulars consider us family, and the feeling is mutual. They share their life struggles and victories with us, and in turn, they want to hear about ours. Their patronage has no limit in value, and we worry about them if we don't see them."

THE AMBIANCE AT THE DINER

The Diner faces the Middlebury green and doesn't look like a classic diner any longer. The façade is a warm yellow paired with red, which is reflected in the large sign featuring a functioning clock that sits over the diner's awning. Walking into the Diner, as with many diners in college towns in Vermont, there is a mixture of generations. You'll find construction workers and locals who have been frequenting the business for years mixed with hung-over college students or those simply looking for a break from campus cafeteria cuisine. The decor inside is more modern than in most classic diners in Vermont. You won't find neon lights and shiny steel but rather reupholstered wooden booths and beams, a black-and-white checkered floor and no counter for service.

Along the west side of the building, a twenty-foot mural of grayscale caricatures was installed in 2015. This unique piece of art was created by Brooklyn-based artist Sarah Grillo, who attended the Gailer School in Shelburne with now owner Harwood. The mural depicts the history of the diner for over forty years, including patrons and owners during the diner's long lifespan. It was designed to commemorate and preserve the rich history of the Diner. "We have something that appeals to all," Harwood said. "Many people have met for the first time at the diner and have begun lifelong relationships as a result of that meeting. Because of this type of history, the mural was painted in its honor. Although we had chosen to make some major changes on the inside of the building, the mural was an attempt to retain some of the best parts of its history."

FOOD AND BEVERAGE AT THE DINER

Open from 7:00 a.m. to 2:00 p.m. seven days a week, the Diner has continued to serve solely breakfast and lunch and serves both all day long. The Diner offers typical eggs, toast and home fries or a hearty BLT sandwich. It has, however, weaved in some eclectic and quirky dishes like the Man-Which, composed of house-braised brisket on a brioche bun with egg and cheddar cheese, or a Biscuit Bomb, consisting of two open-faced biscuits topped with hash browns, two eggs, sausage gravy and cheddar—local, of course. Angry Eggs are a specialty: scrambled eggs with Roesch's homemade South African Hot Sauce, sausage, caramelized onions, tomato and pepper jack.

For those wanting a bit of savory and sweet, the Diner offers half portions of its popular Eggs Benedict over corned beef hash, ham or tomato and spinach, which pair well with a short stack of pancakes, both for $4.99 each. To accommodate all diner-goers, it even specializes in gluten-free pancakes, available in a tall or short stack. "Customers love the pancakes and Belgian waffles. The Nutella French toast is by far the most popular. The Biscuit Bomb is also the top favorite of the egg items," Harwood shared.

To showcase Roesch's South African roots, the lunch menu at the Diner takes a tour around the world with Curry in a Hurry, Roesch's authentic South African chicken curry. A Gyro, Fish and Chips and Chicken and Waffles (or Biscuits) round out the diverse menu, which also offers traditional diner fare with the Ultimate BLT, Patty Melt and Original Reuben. For a touch of fun, the Diner offers the Adirondack Stack, a huge plate of three Vermont beef patties, totaling twenty-four ounces of meat, layered with barbecue sauce, lettuce, tomato, a grilled cheese sandwich and fries. Anyone who can manage to finish this dish receives an "I Beat the Burger at the Diner" T-shirt to celebrate the hefty accomplishment. The Diner and its breakfast and lunch offerings appeal to all age groups, according to Harwood. They see families with young children, young couples, college students and elderly people. The Diner is truly a manifestation of the population of the town, where everyone is welcomed and comes together to share in good company and good food.

Chapter 13

HENRY'S DINER

(802) 862-9010
155 Bank Street
Burlington, Vermont 05401
henrysdinervt.com

AN INTRODUCTION TO BURLINGTON AND HENRY'S DINER

The city of Burlington, Vermont, located in Chittenden County and set on Lake Champlain, is the most populous in Vermont. It is located just forty-five miles south of the Canadian border. Due to the city's proximity to Lake Champlain, it developed into a port of entry for trade in the mid-nineteenth century. Later, Burlington became known as a manufacturing and lumbering center. It is a college town, with the University of Vermont and Champlain College the two main college campuses located near the heart of downtown. Burlington is also a destination for tourists with easy access to Lake Champlain, along with Church Street, a popular brick-lined pedestrian mall with locally owned restaurants, boutiques, art galleries, shops, bars and live music venues. Burlington is a popular town for outdoor recreation as well, with the Burlington Bike Path, a converted walkway from the Center Vermont Railway, offering miles of walking trails along beaches and parks like Leddy Park, Oakledge Park and Battery Park.

Left: Seen here is initial construction for Henry's Diner in Burlington. *Courtesy of Naomi Maglaris and John Couture.*

Below: Today, Henry's Diner is a Burlington staple for locals and tourists alike.

Lake Champlain offers boating, paddle boarding, kayaking and swimming at many of Burlington's beaches and marinas. Burlington is also home to historical sites like the Ethan Allen Homestead Museum, the Fletcher Free Library, the Church Street Historic District, City Hall Park Historic District, a number of churches and chapels and many buildings within the local college campuses.

THE HISTORY OF HENRY'S DINER

Henry's Diner, which sits on Bank Street in Burlington less than a block off Burlington's iconic Church Street, is a vintage, barrel-roofed Jerry O'Mahony diner from 1925 that became disguised as a Spanish-style building during a much later remodel. The dining car itself was transported to Burlington by railroad. The average cost was thought to be $7,500 plus a shipping charge of $325. Henry Couture, the son of Mr. and Mrs. Arthur Couture from Rouses Point, New York, opened the diner in 1925. According to the diner's current menu, this is the full history of the evolution of one of Burlington's most classic eateries:

> *Henry's Diner has been a landmark in the heart of downtown Burlington for more than 90 years. Henry Couture opened Henry's Diner in June 1925. The railroad dining car was brought from Mahony's in Bayonne, New Jersey. The original Henry's had a curved roof, which was a variation from the usual flat-top cars. There was a long counter with the cooking area in front. In those days, the churches and "polite" society looked down their noses at diners. Even the City Fathers gave Henry a hard time before granting him a license. Ladies never stepped inside a diner. Henry changed the image of the dining car. He put window boxes out front and attached striped awnings. Special feminine frills were added to the menu such as waffles, frankfurts, and hamburger on bread that was toasted daintily on one side. Henry won the hearts of the ladies and became the fashionable place to dine on the hill and for ordinary working folk.*
>
> *In June of 1925 under the management of Frank Goldstein, the west wall was opened to provide room for more booths. In 1958, the kitchen area*

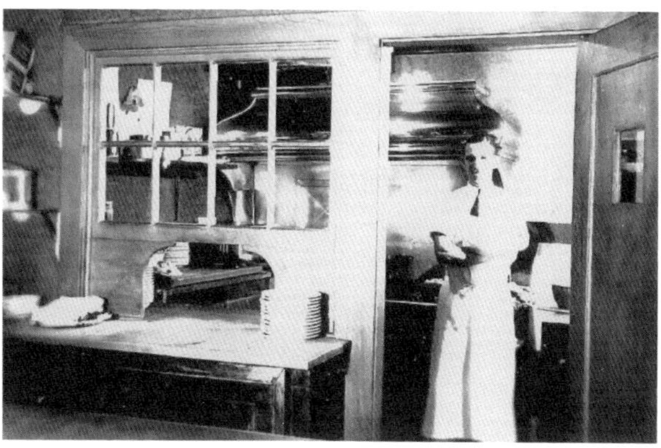

This chef posed in the interior of Henry's Diner in 1924. *Courtesy of Naomi Maglaris and John Couture.*

The diner advertised Hamburger Pattie Sandwiches for fifteen cents. *Courtesy of Naomi Maglaris and John Couture.*

was expanded and more dining space was added. A severe fire on Labor day, September 1, 1969 forced co-owners Frank and Roberta Goldstein to close Henry's Diner temporarily. In spite of the extensive damage, they decided to rebuild. Every effort was made to preserve the imitable charm of Henry's. Improvements such as acoustical ceilings, modern equipment, an attractive décor, and soft background music to enhance the warm intimacy that has always been associated with this home away from home. Henry's re-opened February 21, 1970.

Customers old and new brought their warm wishes for the success of this unique landmark. In March 1982, Frank Goldstein passed away. Their oldest son Harold Michael (called Michael) became general manager. For the next decade or so several members of the Goldstein family operated Henry's. Over the late '90s and early 2000s there were several owners. Bill and Naomi Maglaris and their family came to Henry's in August of 2004. Bill grew up in the restaurant business. His family owned the Arcadia Restaurant on Main Street in Burlington, now known as Reuben James. Bill worked in the kitchen for Holiday Inn during high school and worked his way up the ladder for many years. Bill came with the knowledge and desire to return Henry's back to the well-known diner it used to be; delicious home cooked food at an affordable price in a comfortable atmosphere.

In July of 2014, Henry's closed from July 13th–August 17th for renovations to the front area of the diner so that those with disabilities would have easier access to the restaurant. We look forward to the future knowing that our city is constantly changing. We give thanks to all of our customers and welcome people from diverse countries and cultures. May our customers come in with an appetite and depart happy and satisfied. Welcome to our home. Please come in to relax and enjoy!

Henry's opened its doors in downtown Burlington in 1925. *Courtesy of Naomi Maglaris and John Couture.*

The current owners of Henry's Diner, Naomi and Bill Maglaris, have made it their life mission to preserve the important role the diner has played in the community since 1925. Naomi shared, "My husband grew up in the restaurant business; his family owned and operated family restaurants. When he found out Henry's was for sale, he had the desire to bring it back to the diner it used to be with good-quality, home-cooked food and the type of restaurant he grew up in." She went on, "Henry's is a historical diner. We have put a lot of energy into the old-style dining, from the bright retro decor to the old-style waitress uniforms, service with lots of style and personality, the old-fashioned cash register and the music. We were able to capture that classic Vermont diner atmosphere, and our customers love it."

THE AMBIANCE AT HENRY'S DINER

On a weekend, it's not uncommon to see a line of college students, tourists and locals waiting outside Henry's Diner for a hearty brunch despite many other breakfast options downtown. Henry's has a distinct draw that keeps a diverse crowd coming back for meal after meal. The façade of the building in its current aesthetic doesn't suggest a classic Vermont diner. There's no chrome or stainless steel. In fact, the building itself is covered in a light green stucco in a Mediterranean or Spanish style, with bright green trim. From the exterior, the building doesn't appear to have the long and narrow elongated shape that immediately denotes a diner. Instead, the angular roof makes the diner look taller than most single-story diners. The two

Much of the original layout of Henry's Diner is still the same today. *Courtesy of Naomi Maglaris and John Couture.*

soaring high brick buildings on either side of the diner bring attention to it, as it is small in comparison with a much different look and feel than the rest of the block. The only hint that Henry's is indeed a diner from its exterior is the hanging orange neon sign on a white backdrop suspended over the main door. Old photos of the construction on Henry's showcase its original, more recognizable diner shape.

Upon entering the building, however, Henry's is your quintessential diner in layout, with a color scheme that's unique and notable for classic Vermont diners. Against the windows, yellow-and-gray padded booths line the interior, complemented by yellow counter stools and red-tiled floors. Behind the counter is serving space for the waitresses, who communicate openly with the line cooks who are visible from the front of house. The interior hasn't changed much over time, and the Maglaris family strive to maintain the look and feel of its historical roots in any way they can.

Food and Beverage at Henry's Diner

The Maglarises' favorite part about operating the diners—both Henry's Diner and Athens Diner in Colchester—is the people. It's all about customer stories and customer memories, according to Naomi. She said, "We have something for everyone, and that's what keeps people coming back." The menus at Henry's Diner and the Athens Diner are similar and both extensive. At Henry's, the most popular dishes include homemade Corned Beef Hash, Eggs Benedict, in-house Roasted Turkey, Philly Cheesesteaks, Greek Salad with Chef Bill's secret recipe Greek dressing and the "best Spanakopita in

Chittenden County," according to Naomi, who says the Gyros (pronounced *yeeros*) are also a big hit. Henry's is one of the few diners in Vermont to offer a taste of Greece—that is, Greek platters with Spanakopita, Greek Salad, tzatziki sauce and pita bread. Bill Maglaris is Greek, so the incorporation of Greek fare ties into his own roots.

Named one of America's All-Star Diners by American Express, Henry's has arguably the most extensive diner menu of any classic diner in Vermont, dishing up breakfast and lunch from 6:00 a.m. to 4:00 p.m. Try a milkshake in a variety of flavors, from your classic Chocolate, Chocolate Malt, Vanilla and Strawberry to Chocolate Mint, Mint, Creamsicle, Coffee, Malt, Black and White and Vermont Maple. Floats aren't just limited to Root Beer. At Henry's, you can get your hands on an Orange or Black Cherry Float as well.

Specialties include:

Sausage Gravy over Biscuits: Creamy homemade gravy with crumbled sausage over a buttermilk biscuit. Served with home fries.

Eggs Benedict: Two poached eggs, grilled Canadian bacon on a grilled English muffin, topped with hollandaise sauce. Served with home fries.

Irish Eggs Benedict: Two poached eggs, corned beef hash over a grilled English muffin, all covered in hollandaise. Served with home fries. Or try the Veggie Eggs Benedict with grilled tomato and fresh spinach.

Hungry Henry: Three eggs any style; choice of ham, bacon or sausage; short stack of pancakes or French toast; home fries; and toast, English muffin or biscuit.

Little Henry: The smaller Hungry Henry! Two eggs any style; your choice of ham, bacon or sausage; one pancake or slice of French toast; home fries; and toast, biscuit or English muffin.

Chicken-Fried Steak and Eggs: Steak fried in a crispy batter covered in sausage gravy with two eggs any style; home fries; and toast, biscuit or English muffin.

Steak and Eggs: Grilled strip steak cooked to your liking, served with two eggs, home fries and toast.

Skillets: Served in a cast-iron skillet with home fries, Vermont cheddar, topped with two eggs of any style and served with toast, biscuit or English muffin.

The Role of Henry's Diner in the Local Community

Henry's Diner is one of Vermont's classic diners that showcases the commonality among patrons, since it attracts such a diverse crowd. Henry's is a huge draw for college students, as well as locals. Like many diners in Vermont that play a significant role in their local communities, Henry's Diner donates to many nonprofit organizations in Burlington and around Vermont. Naomi stated, "We are a meeting place for locals, and we draw in people from all walks of life. Henry's is special because of the memories and customer experiences. All generations love coming for the ambiance. We are a rarity. In our minds, the nostalgic atmosphere makes Henry's special. Burlington has experienced all kinds of historical events over the last ninety-three years, and Henry's has been here for all of it! We are a landmark in downtown Burlington."

Christina Aftonomos, a Burlington resident, shared, "I love the atmosphere, the fast and friendly service and the feeling of community there. There are some places that draw in a particular crowd (college kids, young professionals, etc.), but the crowd at Henry's is so diverse. It's always nice to find a place that recognizes you as a familiar face after just a few visits, too! There's always a line out the door on the weekends, which tells me that so many people in the community feel the same way I do."

Chapter 14

THE ATHENS DINER

(802) 655-3455
46 Highpoint Center
Colchester, Vermont 05446

AN INTRODUCTION TO COLCHESTER AND THE ATHENS DINER

Colchester, Vermont, is home to more than seventeen thousand residents and is the second most populous town in Chittenden County. Located just to the north of Burlington, Colchester is situated to the east of Lake Champlain and to the west of the Green Mountains. It sits on Malletts Bay of Lake Champlain and is a community rooted in outdoor recreation, with many marinas lining the shores of the lake. Colchester is also home to Airport Park and the Colchester Causeway Trail, a nearly eleven-mile walking and bike path that allows runners, bikers and walkers to take in the sights and smells of the lake. Visitors can even take a bike ferry from one part of the causeway to the next section to access the second portion of the trail. Colchester regularly makes the list of the best places to live in Vermont for the family-friendliness, safety and quality of life it affords. Colchester is also one of many college towns in Vermont, home to Saint Michael's College. College students are known to cozy up into a booth at the Athens Diner and study over coffee and pie or a hearty meal. Colchester also is home to one of the

The Athens Diner, Worcester #838, sits high above the town of Colchester.

few drive-in theaters still in operation in Vermont, on Porters Point Road. Ernest and Dorothy Handy bought the Sunset Drive-In from a developer in 1948, and it has been in operation since then, playing a significant role in the Colchester community and the preservation of the drive-in culture. Sunset Drive-In, which now has four big screens, has a retro, nostalgic draw for locals and tourists alike, much like the Athens Diner.

THE HISTORY OF THE ATHENS DINER

Naomi and Bill Maglaris, who are the wife-and-husband team that also owns Henry's Diner in downtown Burlington, had the goal of running multiple classic diners in Vermont. At one point, the diner duo owned four diners close to one another in Vermont: Henry's; Arcadia Diner in South Burlington, now known as the Parkway Diner; Apollo Diner in Milton; and Athena's Diner in St. Albans. Neither the Apollo Diner nor Athena's Diner is still in operation. The Arcadia Diner, which was named after a restaurant Bill Maglaris's grandfather owned and operated next to the Flynn Theater in Burlington, ran into lease issues and closed after five years. Since then, the iconic "airport diner" has been reopened by chef Corey Gottfried, who worked in the Maglarises' diner kitchens for over ten years.

Libby's Blue Line Diner operated in its hilltop location on Route 7 close to Interstate 89 in Colchester for twenty-two years before it was sold to the Maglarises in 2012. Before coming to Vermont, the diner operated as the Casu Diner in Turner's Falls, Massachusetts, starting in 1953 and then later as the Forest Diner in Auburn, Massachusetts, starting in the early 1960s. In 1989, the classic dining car came to Vermont, where it became known as Libby's Blue Line Diner and was owned by Karen Griffin, who owned and operated Libby's with her mother, Elizabeth "Libby" Griffin. In 2012, the Maglarises took ownership of the 1940s diner car located on a hilltop overlooking Colchester, at which point it was renamed the Athens Diner, tying into Bill's Greek roots. The Athens Diner car itself is a Worcester Lunch Car Company, #838, and was one the last diners built by the diner manufacturer.

The Ambiance at the Athens Diner

The exterior of the Athens Diner denotes a classic diner with ample metal, a black-and-red alternating tile border around white tile and windows lining the building. The building might seem more elongated than a classic diner car, and it is. Two extensions on either end flank the historic Worcester dining car. Although the words "Athens Diner" appear on the façade in a Greek-inspired font, the original "Blue Line Diner" words remain intact. Inside, the interior has red-and-blue stools and plenty of booths alongside the windows. The layout of the diner is your typical Worcester Lunch Car Company layout, with counter seating with chrome-and-red letter banded stools and wooden booths by the windows. On the floor, you'll see an intricate black-and-white tiled motif, along with tiles lining the counter in the traditional Art Deco style. Take note of the chrome detailing behind the counter and above the waitress work stations.

Food and Drink at the Athens Diner

At the Athens, the menu is similar to Henry's Diner downtown but features more extensive Greek food and more vegetarian options. Breakfast is served

The Athens Diner was originally home to Libby's Blue Line Diner in the same location.

all day. The portions are large, and the prices remain fair. Crowd favorites are the Buttermilk Pancakes, Belgian Waffle, Sausage and Gravy over fluffy biscuits and the Irish Eggs Benedict (two poached eggs over homemade corned beef hash on an English muffin topped with hollandaise sauce and served with home fries). The Athens Diner offers a range of traditional diner sandwiches, including Tuna Salad, Chicken Salad, Egg Salad, Corned Beef, Egg and Olive, Minute Steak, Clam Roll, Ham and Cheese, Roast Beef, Ham, the classic BLT and Turkey Reuben. Clubs are a favorite diner food, and the Athens offers six versions of the classic sandwich. In addition to the Turkey Club, served with Adams' Turkey Farm turkey, triple layered with bacon, lettuce and tomato, the diner also serves up a Chicken Salad Club, Roast Pork Loin Club, Roast Beef or Ham Club, Tuna Salad Club and even Hamburger Club with Angus beef.

Eleven burgers grace the menu. The Cordon Bleu Burger is topped with shaved ham and cheese. The Italian Burger is topped with homemade marinara and provolone. The Western Burger is topped with barbecue sauce, onion rings and cheddar cheese. The Spanish Burger is topped with the diner's homemade Spanish sauce and cheddar cheese. There's even a Lamb Burger, with fresh ground lamb served with lettuce, tomato and onions and topped with their special Greek yogurt garlic sauce. Complete Meals—which come with soup, your choice of potato, vegetable and roll and butter—are diner classics, from Country-Fried Steak, Shepard's Pie and Meatloaf to Pork Chops, Ham Steak, Liver and Onions and Hand-Cut Sirloin Steak. Don't miss the Roasted Vermont Turkey Dinner with sage stuffing and cranberry sauce for the ultimate comfort food.

Bill Maglaris's Greek influence shines through as well. He offers the Santorini Breakfast Sandwich (fried eggs with spinach, tomato and feta cheese on grilled Greek bread), along with the Athens Breakfast skillet (grilled home fries topped with grilled spinach and caramelized onions and topped with feta cheese and two eggs). Under Greek Specials, the Athens offers a variety of Gyros, from the Lamb Gyro (fresh ground beef and lamb served on pita bread with tzatziki sauce, lettuce, tomatoes and onions) to a Chicken Gyro or Souvlaki Gyro (marinated pork tenderloin). The Greek-inspired portion of the menu also offers Moussaka (a Greek lasagna), a Spanakopita Platter (spinach pie served with Greek salad, handmade pita bread and tzatziki) and a Greek Platter (choice of lamb, chicken or souvlaki with spinach pie, Greek salad, handmade pita bread and tzatziki).

The varied vegetarian options receive rave reviews from patrons, as traditionally diners are quite heavy on meat products. The Veggie Skillet is a big hit, with grilled home fries, mushrooms, onion, peppers and tomatoes topped with cheddar cheese and two eggs. Most omelets are vegetarian, including the Vegetarian Omelet itself (mushrooms, tomatoes, bell peppers and onions) and the Spanish Omelet (tomatoes, onions, bell peppers, black bean salsa and cheddar). There's also a Veggie Wrap with lettuce, tomato, onions, mushrooms and cucumbers in a flour wrap. As so much stays the same at diners, many roadside eateries in Vermont are adapting to different dietary preferences and restrictions, keeping with the accommodating nature of diners and their willingness to ensure all can eat and enjoy.

Desserts are extensive at the Athens Diner, with fresh baked pies, assorted Jell-O and puddings, cream pies, cakes, pastries and Baklava to finish a Greek meal. They also have an ice cream shop and serve up the "World's Smallest Sundae"—a guiltless dessert for seventy-nine cents, which includes ice cream with hot fudge, strawberries, pineapple, caramel, whipped cream and a cherry. Milkshakes are available in chocolate, vanilla, strawberry or orange cream, along with old-fashioned chocolate malts and ice cream floats with root beer, orange cream soda, black cherry soda and grape soda.

Chapter 15

PARKWAY DINER

(802) 652-1155
1696 Williston Road
South Burlington, Vermont 05403

AN INTRODUCTION TO SOUTH BURLINGTON AND THE PARKWAY DINER

Located in western Chittenden County, South Burlington is the second-largest city in Vermont, bordering Winooski, Essex, Colchester and Shelburne, along with Lake Champlain to the west. The city is home to Burlington International Airport, just around the corner from the Parkway Diner, and the base for the Vermont Air National Guard and the Vermont Army National Guard. The town was organized in 1785 but was incorporated in 1865, at which time Burlington was also chartered as a city. Now home to nearly twenty thousand residents, South Burlington is a service-based economy with a range of retail businesses and Vermont's largest shopping mall, the University Mall. The town also boasts a number of scenic parks for outdoor recreation, including Red Rocks Park, Overlook Park, Jaycee Park and Wheeler Nature Park, along with the iconic Whales Tales, which can be seen while driving northbound on Interstate 89. Higher Ground, the region's go-to venue for live music, is also on Williston Road, one of the main roads in South Burlington's retail section.

THE HISTORY OF THE PARKWAY DINER

Also located on Williston Road in South Burlington, close to the Burlington International Airport, the Parkway Diner is a Worcester Lunch Car Company diner car, #839, dating to 1953. Worcester Lunch Car Company only made eleven more diner cars after this one. The Parkway Diner was moved to South Burlington from Worcester, Massachusetts, in 1955. It was purchased by Gus and George Lines, who owned it until 1970. At that time, it was purchased by George Hagen and later leased by George and Christine Alvanos, who ran the diner for ten years until Bill Maglaris purchased it. Alvanos, who had been in Vermont since 1980, was of Greek descent and expanded the diner's menu to include a variety of Greek fare, such as moussaka, spanakopita, gyros and other popular Greek dishes. The current owner and chef, Corey Gottfried, grew up working in diners in Vermont, including under the previous owner of the then Arcadia Diner, Maglaris, who now owns Henry's Diner in Burlington and the Athens Diner in Colchester.

THE AMBIANCE AT THE PARKWAY DINER

From the exterior, the Parkway Diner looks like a vintage dining car with a red metal and stainless façade, along with a black-and-white awning. The diner car stands alone in a parking lot and draws guests in through an oversized neon sign that's rustic and historic, with the word "Diner" illuminated in bright orange. Inside the Parkway Diner, almost everything remains intact from its original state. The wooden booths against the windows are lined with red cushions, matching the counter stools and tiled trim along the outer walls. The floor is an intricately tiny-tiled design of pink and brown accents. The stools at the counter, which have been seating guests for over half a century at the roadside eatery, are chrome-banded and topped with red leather. The counters themselves are well-worn and well-loved Formica and barely have a hint of the original pattern left intact. Look up and see the curved roofline of the dining car, which was a standard in Worcester Lunch Car Company manufactured diners. Inside, you'll also find an original Worcester dining car clock, as well as stained-glass windows depicting the diner in blue and yellow and a lake scene. Black moveable letter announcement boards with white lettering above the workspace and cooktop share the sources of local ingredients used in

Above: The Parkway Diner in South Burlington is located by Burlington International Airport and often referred to as the Airport Diner.

Left: The interior of the Parkway Diner boasts warm wooden booths.

the food at the diner. From eggs and bacon to maple syrup and vegetables, the Parkway Diner—like many other Vermont diners—strives to utilize ingredients from neighboring farms and producers. The Parkway Diner is one of few classic diners in Vermont with a line for preparing food on the other side of the counter. This adds to the camaraderie and friendship that is evident when seated in the space. Locals chat with Gottfried and the line cooks, truly getting to know one another. The Parkway Diner is one of the most lively and energized diners in Vermont, likely due to the proximity of the cooks and staff to the patrons themselves.

FOOD AND BEVERAGE AT THE PARKWAY DINER

Gottfried, who worked at a number of diners and restaurants in Vermont over the span of twenty years, including Denny's and the University of Vermont Medical Center, produces some of the best-quality old-fashioned, homemade meals of all Vermont diners. The classic diner menu is one of the smaller in the state but with ample care to prepare flavorful meals, some of which have slight twists on traditional diner fare in their preparation. For his Corned Beef Hash, he slow roasts a brisket that he then breaks down. He's also known for his Homemade Seitan for vegetarian customers, along with his thick and creamy Sausage Gravy over cheddar biscuits and Hot Turkey Sandwich, served with hand-cut French fries and thick gravy.

On the breakfast menu, dishes are steeped in tradition, such as the Breakfast Sandwich (grilled English muffin; one egg over hard; cheese; choice of bacon, sausage patties or Canadian bacon; served with home fries). Cinnamon French Toast with bacon, sausage, ham or pancake is classic but a perennial favorite. For omelets, the Parkway Diner offers traditional filling options: Plain, Cheese, Ham and Cheese, Western and Vegetable. The Two Eggs (Any Style) over homemade corned beef hash with home fries and choice of thick-sliced toast are the staple dish for breakfast, with locals, regulars and tourists regularly complimenting the peppery and flavor-bursting hash. Two Eggs (Any Style) with hand-carved rib-eye steak with home fries and toast is another hearty staple of the diner's breakfast menu.

The lunch menu is as classic diner as it comes, with sandwiches ranging from Ham and Roast Turkey to Roast Beef, Chicken Salad, Grilled Cheese, Tuna Salad, Egg Salad, a Western and a BLT—all ranging in price from $5.95 to $6.25 and served with pickle slices and chips. On the griddle are

The extensive menu at the Parkway Diner boasts eggs of all kinds, burgers, Reubens, turkey clubs and more traditional diner fare.

burgers served with coleslaw and hand-cut seasoned potatoes. The Vermont Burger boasts apple slices, cheddar and bacon, whereas the Spicy Burger is topped with grilled onions, jalapeños, and pepper jack. On all burgers, a second juicy burger patty can be added for $2.65. The open-faced hot sandwiches are comfort food goodness, such as a Roast Turkey Sandwich and Pork Tenderloin Sandwich over white bread with gravy, with a slide of homemade mashed potatoes and coleslaw, of course.

THE ROLE OF THE PARKWAY DINER IN THE LOCAL COMMUNITY

The mixture of regulars, locals and college students makes the Parkway Diner a destination for all kinds. Regulars have been eating at the diner for fifteen to thirty-five years. During that time, they've seen the owners of the diner change and the menus evolve, but the space has stayed the same.

Some regulars come in for a bowl of Cheerios and a coffee or perhaps a buttered English muffin on the grill. Others come in for oatmeal and the companionship, of course. For many, the Parkway Diner is an institution in their lives. The diner has become a familiar part of their lives and a habitual routine. According to Cody Vernet, who lives and works in the area, "While I'm not a regular, whenever I visit the Parkway, it always seems like it is full of regular customers who use the Parkway as a meeting point to meet up and discuss community events and news. It is also a good place to hold a meeting with a coworker or client, especially during the week when it is less busy." He went on, "The Parkway brings people together through its tight setting. The bar that runs along the front of the diner allows for open mingling between patrons. It is in a classic diner car and has the look and feel I want in a diner experience. I grew up loving classic diners and was extremely excited when I found the Parkway just down the road from my house."

Vernet continued, "I think millennials seek out experiences more than any other generation. They want a place that not only has good food but also provides an experience along with the meal. I think diners, specifically those still operating out of classic diner cars, provide the experience they are looking for. Many people go out to breakfast and diners on the weekends, often making them packed, hard to get into, and create a long wait for a seat. The true magic of a diner, and the time I love to go, is during the weekdays. Going to a diner on any given Tuesday at 9:00 a.m. provides a pleasant, quiet dining experience that you cannot find on the weekend. While there is a nice nostalgic feeling of starting off Saturday with a trip to the diner or a long brunch on Sunday morning, the real magical time is during the workweek. The diners are quieter, the food is just as good and the feeling is truly relaxing, as you do not feel rushed by other patrons waiting for a seat as you could on the weekend. Whenever I have to travel out of state during the week, I always start my trip at the Parkway Diner and look forward to coming back to it."

Chapter 16

MISS LYNDONVILLE DINER

(802) 626-9890
686 Broad Street
Lyndonville, Vermont 05851

AN INTRODUCTION TO LYNDONVILLE AND THE MISS LYNDONVILLE DINER

Lyndonville, located in the town of Lyndon in Caledonia County in Vermont, is a village of less than one square mile with a population of 1,200 residents. The village was incorporated in in 1880. Lyndon spans approximately six square miles and is often celebrated as one of the most beautiful areas in Vermont, due to the amount of open space and wildlife. Close to St. Johnsbury and Newport, Lyndonville is part of the Northeast Kingdom in Vermont and is home to Lyndon State College, a public liberal arts college that also offers a variety of master's programs, along with Lyndon Institute. The Northeast Kingdom is a region of fifty-five towns in northeast Vermont, containing Caledonia, Essex and Orleans Counties. The NEK, as it's referred to, is home to Jay Peak, the summit of the Green Mountains and also Jay Peak Resort and the Burke Mountain ski area and is bordered by the Connecticut River and is close to Lake Willoughby. The area is known as being pastoral and rural, with extensive wildlife in the area, including moose, deer, black bears, wild turkeys, coyotes and bobcats. Additionally,

Lyndon and the Northeast Kingdom at large are known for being home to a number of Vermont's covered bridges, including the Randall Bridge (1865), School House Bridge (1879), Chamberlain Mill Bridge (1881), Sanborn Run Bridge (1869) and Millers Run Bridge (1995). The plethora of covered bridges paired with the beauty of the region brings visitors to the Northeast Kingdom for rest and relaxation, outdoor recreation and photography of wildlife, covered bridges and the rural landscape.

THE HISTORY OF THE MISS LYNDONVILLE DINER

The Miss Lyndonville Diner, a Sterling dining car circa 1939, sits on Route 5 in Lyndonville and is one of few eateries in the quaint Northeast Kingdom community and college town. Articles about it in the *Boston Globe*, the *New York Times* and local publications like *Vermont Magazine* have contributed to the popularity of the eatery. The diner opened in 1951 and was purchased by Janet Gray Burnor and her now late husband, Ashley, in 1978. When Janet and Ashley purchased the diner, it was called Rustic Restaurant. Before that, it was called the Miss Lynn Diner. Since then, it's been a family affair, as is the case with many diners in Vermont. When they started the diner, there were only eight items in the menu; now there are countless dishes, with one of the most diverse and extensive menus among Vermont's classic diners.

In 1979, the diner experienced a fire and was largely gutted. In the aftermath of the fire, Janet and Ashley chose to rebuild and expand the size of the diner to offer affordable diner fare to more guests at once. Although the Sterling diner isn't recognizable as such from the exterior after more than half a century of renovations, inside, the diner is as classic as they come.

THE AMBIANCE AT THE MISS LYNDONVILLE DINER

The original diner has been enclosed by wood frames, not appearing to be a classic Vermont diner from the white exterior that resembles a typical family restaurant located close to the roadside. Red awnings and flower boxes accentuate the windows and add a welcoming touch. The words "Miss Lyndonville Diner" appear over the windows in red feminine script

The interior of Miss Lyndonville is bright and welcoming, with counter stools and booth service.

font. By the entrance, a piece of bicycle art adds to the uniqueness of the façade. American and Canadian flags fly high over the building. Inside, the Miss Lyndonville Diner is recognizable as a quintessential diner with a rounded ceiling, cushy booths and a long lunch counter with stools. There's ample light pouring into the space and artwork of other classic diners in Vermont by local artists. The interior is homey and warm, with more wood throughout than is typical in a diner. There's also more space, leading to a less cramped yet still intimate gathering space. The black and chrome stools sit against a wooden backdrop and a newer green countertop. Behind the counter are the coffee and work stations with classic chrome and stainless steel overhead. The mugs are classic diner, with a faded green representation of the diner with a quote from *Yankee Magazine*: "A really great place for enthusiastic eaters of all ages." There's an opening to the kitchen, which is seen from the front of the diner but operates behind the scenes. A second room also in warm yellow paint—part of the addition—extends the dining car and adds capacity to the popular eatery.

FOOD AND BEVERAGE AT THE MISS LYNDONVILLE DINER

The menu from the Miss Lyndonville showcases traditional diner fare in a classic Vermont diner setting.

Breakfast is served all day every day, and the menu features over thirty-seven different breakfast items. With such an expansive menu, all dishes are numbered to make ordering easier. Sweet breakfast favorites include Strawberry Pancakes and Blueberry Pancake Rollups, Stuffed French Toast filled with orange marmalade cream cheese, Cinnamon Bread French Toast and the Hot Berry French Toast, which includes two slices of French toast topped with ice cream and strawberries. Savory breakfast favorites include the Skillet Breakfast (a biscuit and sausage gravy, home fries, two strips of bacon and an egg), the Ham Steak Breakfast (a half pound of ham steak with two eggs, home fries and homemade toast), the Country-Fried Steak breakfast (breaded beef steak, country gravy, home fries, two eggs and toast) and Corned Beef Hash (served with two eggs and a grilled corn muffin).

For lunch and dinner guests, Miss Lyndonville serves up a variety of classic diner dishes, like a Hot Turkey or Hot Pot Roast Sandwich, Homestyle Meat Loaf or an American Spaghetti Diner. Sandwiches and platters get more inventive beyond traditional diner staples, including the Swiss Lad (baked ham, melted Swiss cheese, lettuce, tomato and special sauce on a hoagie roll), the Chicken Mozzarella Pita (grilled chicken breast, melted mozzarella, lettuce, tomato and ranch dressing), the Vermonter (a five-ounce grilled beef patty served open face on a toasted roll with steak fries and beef gravy) or the delicious Three Decker Hamburger and Cheese Club (five ounces of ground beef, American cheese, bacon, lettuce, tomato, onion and gravy). Desserts include Strawberry Pie and Blueberry Pie, a homemade Cream Pie of the Day, Pecan Pie, Apple Pie, Carrot Cake, Strawberry Shortcake, Cheese Cake, Jell-O, pudding and Hot Fudge Ice Cream Cake. Coffee refills are ample, and a slice of pie from the dessert case is offered at the end of every meal by attentive waitresses, quick to flash a warm smile.

THE ROLE OF THE MISS LYNDONVILLE DINER IN THE LOCAL COMMUNITY

The Miss Lyndonville Diner emphasizes service and fosters interactions between the workers and guests. It has been an institution in the small Vermont community for decades. It's no surprise that the Miss Lyndonville is well loved and regarded by regulars, locals, college students and tourists to the village. Hannah Manley, a 1997 graduate of Lyndon State College and Miss Vermont in 2000, shared, "The Miss Lyndonville Diner is central to the Lyndonville community. On any given day, you can find a mix of locals—most natives of the Northeast Kingdom, Lyndon State College students and those just passing through. The diner has been run by the same family for decades, and it hasn't changed—in a good way." Manley continued, "The menu I remember as a college student more than twenty years ago is the same menu I see today. Lyndon State College students quickly learn that the Miss Lyndonville is the place to go to get a break from cafeteria food. Breakfast all day is a huge draw for college students—delicious and totally affordable. Tried-and-true main dishes include the pot roast, hamburgers and the chicken mozzarella pita. And don't forget the cream pies. If you've run out of room, simply get it to go. When Lyndon State College alumni return to campus for homecoming or reunion and bring their families back to see their alma mater, a trip to the Miss Lyndonville is at the top of everyone's priority list....And they are always comforted by the fact that it has remained the same—in the best possible way."

Mary Jane Russell, a native of Lyndonville, recounted, "When [now husband] Gary and I were newly dating, I brought him back home from college to meet my family. After a big meal Friday night, my dad [longtime Lyndonville resident Doug Beans] asked the new boyfriend, 'Would you like to go out to breakfast at the diner in the morning?' As most young male college students would do, he knew better than to refuse a big country breakfast—especially one at the famed Miss Lyndonville. 'Great,' my dad said," Russell continued. "'We'll meet the boys at the diner at 6:00 a.m.' That was not, of course, part of a typical college student's Saturday morning routine! Gary was a good sport and went out for breakfast, but then Dad took him to our sugarhouse, where he and the boys worked in the woods all day long. Thinking that must be a fluke, because surely they had cut enough wood last time to fuel the entire Northeast Kingdom's spring sugaring operations, Gary fell for it the next time he visited as well: a big breakfast, but then worked in the woods cutting firewood all day long."

Russell continued to recount, "The third time, being the smart college student that he was, Gary was anticipating the breakfast offer and preemptively responded, 'Oh, no thanks, I had such a big dinner; I'll be full for days! I think I'll pass on breakfast tomorrow.' 'Okay,' my father replied hesitantly, 'I guess we can sleep in instead. We'll meet the boys at 6:30 a.m. and go straight over to the sugarhouse.'" Gary should have chosen another hearty breakfast at the Miss Lyndonville to fuel his day. Like many locals, the diner has become a standard in their lives and an integral part of the community of which it has become such a big part.

Chapter 17

A ROAD TRIP TO VERMONT'S CLASSIC DINERS

A classic activity in any season in Vermont is the road trip. Vermonters and visitors to the Green Mountain State take to the scenic roads winding throughout Vermont—over mountain gaps, across farmland and around lakes—to take in the natural beauty that Vermont has become known for. In a state with no large cities and little traffic, traveling by car is the norm and an activity in and of itself. The allure of road-tripping is finding new discoveries that make for new adventures along the way. Fall in Vermont is the most popular season for road-tripping. Tourists flock to Vermont and New England to leaf peep—taking in the orange, red and gold of the changing fall color. In the winter, locals and tourists head for the mountains in any weather conditions to get first tracks. During the spring, as the frost in the ground thaws, Vermont's main roads become bumpy with frost heaves, and back roads turn to mud—defining the fifth season in Vermont. Even during mud season, though, locals begin to stir after a long winter with the promise of spring in the not-too-far-off distance. In summer, when days are long and sunshine is copious, Vermont's roads lead locals and visitors to hike the Long Trail, boat on Lake Champlain or take a drive with no destination in mind—the very best kind of road trip and where the best memories are made.

Throughout the state, there are scenic byways that showcase Vermont's natural intrigue. The Molly Stark Scenic Byway runs on Route 9 for 48 miles from Brattleboro to Bennington. The Shires of Vermont Byway is a route between the Green Mountains and Taconic Mountains on Route

Miss Lyndonville's original diner structure has been framed in, so it looks more like a restaurant from the exterior.

7A. Bookended by the two shire towns of Bennington and Manchester, this byway has long mountain views and runs parallel to the Long Trail. The Stone Valley Scenic Byway takes drivers on Route 30 for 30 miles, through Hubbardton, Castleton, Poultney, Wells, Pawlet, Rupert, Manchester and Dorset—quintessential Vermont small towns. The Connecticut River National Byway follows the Connecticut River on Route 91 in Vermont through Brattleboro, Bellows Falls, Windsor, White River Junction, Wells River and St. Johnsbury. The Lake Champlain Byway runs 134 miles from Middlebury to Vergennes, Burlington and the Champlain Islands following Route 7 and Route 2, with views of mountains, lakes, farms and quaint town centers. The Mad River Scenic Byway, one of the most stunning and popular road trip routes in Vermont, runs for 35 miles on Routes 100 and 100B through Granville, Warren, Waitsfield, Moretown and Middlesex, by farms, famous ski towns and historic sites. The Green Mountain Byway is 11 miles in length, running from Waterbury to Stowe, bringing drivers close to Vermont's ski country, breweries and some of the state's best outdoor recreation. Along the majority of these scenic byways, road trippers will stumble upon welcoming signs for Vermont's classic diners and roadside eateries that will beckon them, pulling them inside for a unique dining experience.

In Vermont, in addition to scenic byways that act as guides to travel the state, there are also many "trails" that showcase the best made-in-Vermont products and local experiences throughout the Green Mountain State. The Vermont Beer Passport, started by the Vermont Brewers Association with the slogan "Beer Worth Finding," challenges beer lovers to hit the beer trail to discover new styles of beer and breweries throughout the state. The Vermont Cheese Trail, launched by the Vermont Cheese Council, showcases cheesemakers and their unique processes and products with interactive and printable maps of cheesemakers and others offering farm tours and retail sales that are open to the public. Vermont also boasts a wine trail called the International Champlain Valley Wine Trail, which includes winery destinations in Vermont, on the New York side of Lake Champlain and even in Quebec, Canada. During sap season in the late winter and early spring when days warm up and nights are still cold, many sugarhouses in Vermont also host open houses, creating a maple syrup trail across the state. At some times during the year, farms host open farm weekends, and artisans throughout the state also open up their galleries, pottery studios and woodworking studios for a gallery tour of the state. Traveling through Vermont with or without a defined purpose is always enjoyable, more so with good company and the promise of a new discovery along the way.

With a number of classic diners still in operation in Vermont, why not take a road trip to visit the state's best, most authentic roadside eateries rooted in history and get to know the ins and outs of Vermont in the process? Vermont's classic diners are spread out throughout the state, encouraging widespread exploration. When visiting Vermont's diners in a short period of time, the nuances of each historic dining car design stand out. You're able to appreciate how distinct elements of the interior or exterior are and how other things all look the same. You can begin to appreciate how many diners in Vermont have withstood the test of time with only hints of their age—displayed mostly through worn Formica countertops showing the imprints of many elbows lining the lunch counters for three meals a day and chips in tiled flooring with miles walked over them throughout the years. It's a fun process to compare the color schemes and tile patterns and to see how some diners, like the Birdseye in Castleton, Chelsea Royal Diner in Brattleboro or Miss Lyndonville in Lyndonville, have expanded their capacity, while others have preserved the tiny—and now often crowded—interiors of traditional dining cars, like the Blue Benn in Bennington or the Parkway Diner in South Burlington. With so many similar dishes served across the state at classic diners, a road trip is the best way to find the best corned beef hash, hamburger, BLT, club sandwich or other go-to traditional diner fare.

THE ULTIMATE VERMONT CLASSIC DINER ROAD TRIP ITINERARY

In order to eat your way through most, if not all, of Vermont at the state's classic diners, it's important to be strategic when mapping out your diner road trip. You need to build in recovery time to prepare yourself for your next meal and ensure you also allow for time at historic sites and general Vermont attractions along your route. Part of the joy and excitement of road-tripping on Vermont's country roads is being able to pull over suddenly and spontaneously to admire a waterfall, peruse the eclectic offerings in a general store, taste a flight of beers at a local craft brewery or stroll leisurely through diverse town centers, popping in and out of boutiques, galleries and other locally owned shops. When crafting an epic road trip itinerary, building in time for spur-of-the-moment decisions of new destinations is important. From a local and frequent road tripper in Vermont, here is a guide to visiting Vermont's classic diners, while getting to know the brand that is Vermont through local activities, products and Vermont's best attribute: its people, who embody the community-minded spirit that defines the state.

The back of the Blue Benn boasts a unique yellow and blue sign.

Coming into Vermont from the south, make your way to Bennington for a morning visit to the Blue Benn, one of Vermont's most well-known diners. Take your time. Don't be rushed. You likely will have to wait for a seat in the tiny diner. Enjoy one of the Blue Benn's signature vegetarian dishes, a grilled corn muffin or one of many types of pancakes. While in Bennington, visit the Bennington Battle Monument and Bennington Museum for some local history, and then go on the hunt for two covered bridges: the Silk Road Covered Bridge and Burt Henry Covered Bridge. Begin to make your way from Bennington to Brattleboro along Route 9, the Molly Stark Scenic Byway—about an hour in length, with the occasional pull-off for a scenic overlook or stop along the route. For a late lunch or, if you're still full from breakfast, ice cream or a Vermont creemee, stop at the Chelsea Royal Diner in Brattleboro. The diner has some of the best curb appeal of any diner in Vermont and an extensive menu full of diner favorites and twists on the originals. The Clam Roll is a crowd favorite for lunch, with seafood brought in regularly to the southern Vermont eatery.

In Brattleboro, visit the Creamery Covered Bridge and walk the downtown to get a sense for the community steeped in culture, history and art. In the late afternoon, visit Hermit Thrush Brewery, one of Vermont's brewers known for its sour-style beers, or Saxtons River Distillery for a sample of its unique Vermont-made libations. Take the Shires of Vermont Byway from Bennington to Manchester, home for the night. In Manchester, choose to stay at an iconic resort like the Equinox Golf Resort and Spa or a locally owned inn like the Inn at Manchester or the Hill Farm Hill in Sunderland, a rural setting outside town. For a budget-friendly option, spend the night at the Manchester View or the Stamford Motel and Restaurant. In the morning, make your way to Bob's Diner on the outskirts of town, where Routes 11 and 30 meet. At Bob's, enjoy a hearty breakfast skillet or a twist on Eggs Benedict with a smoked salmon and dill Hollandaise sauce version in the company of doting servers, eager to make your day. Grab a coffee to go to fuel your next adventure along your Vermont road trip. For history buffs, visit Hildene, the home and gardens of the Lincoln family. For outdoor enthusiasts, hike Lye Brook Falls or visit the American Museum of Fly Fishing. For the deal-hunter, visit the Manchester Designer Outlets, and don't miss the Northshire Bookstore, one of the oldest and most iconic book shops in Vermont. In time for a late lunch, drive Route 7 from Manchester to Castleton for an hour, stopping at the H.N. Williams Store in Dorset for a quintessential Vermont country store experience. Just up the road from H.N. Williams, pull off to admire the Dorset Marble Quarry, a popular swimming hole and cliff-jumping spot for locals in the summer months. Wind your way through Rutland into the college town of Castleton, where the Birdseye Diner awaits for a lunch or dinner meal. At the Birdseye, belly up to the lunch counter for a juicy burger or breakfast special. Don't forget to try a Malted Milkshake or the Egg Cream from the malt shop while there. As a souvenir of your trip, purchase one of the Birdseye's iconic yellow mugs for ten dollars; if you don't, you'll regret it as soon as you leave. For your resting spot for the night, drive forty minutes north via Route 30 through farmland and along country roads to Middlebury, another quaint college town and home to The Diner on Merchants Row.

In Middlebury, stay at the Middlebury Inn, overlooking the green in the center of town, or the Swift House Inn just up the road. Both inns are rooted in Vermont history and still maintain an essence of simpler times. The next morning, wake up and take a stroll through town to The Diner, formerly known as Steve's Park Diner. Although it might not look like a classic diner from the façade, spend time studying the mural inside and reading the articles that line the walls. Enjoy a traditional diner breakfast, fuel for your next activity. Check out Middlebury College's campus, the Otter Creek Falls downtown and the Pulp Mill Covered Bridge first before leaving the quintessential Vermont college town. Next, spend the morning hiking Snake Mountain, a four-mile easy-to-moderate trail following an Old Carriage Road, to stretch your legs, make more room for sustenance and take in the stunning views of the Adirondack Mountains and Vermont's pristine farmland from the top. If hiking isn't an attraction, head north up Route 7 to Vermont's smallest city, Vergennes, and stroll through the quaint downtown, visiting Daily Chocolate and the Vergennes Laundry bake shop. Continue north up to Burlington, the headquarters for your next night (or two) in Vermont on the Green Mountain Byway.

In Ferrisburgh on Route 7, you'll see Ollie, a camel in Vermont. Yes, a camel that is a Vermont attraction and a sight to see. In Burlington, make your way to Henry's Diner, an iconic downtown eatery since 1925. With one of the most extensive menus of all diners in Vermont, it also boasts authentic Greek fare. Take in the bright interior with yellow booths and stools and the classically dressed waitresses, always serving guests with a smile. Turn right to Church Street and explore the pedestrian mall, or turn left and walk down to the Burlington bike path to take in the sights and smells of Lake Champlain. Or visit Pine Street in Burlington, where craft breweries abound, for a pub crawl through town. For an evening meal, head to El Cortijo Taqueria y Cantina down Bank Street from Henry's Diner. El Cortijo is housed in a classic dining car and previously was known as the Oasis Diner. There are a number of hotels downtown, including Hotel Vermont, the only independently owned hotel in Burlington, and historic bed-and-breakfasts within walking distance of downtown, including the Lang House on Main Street Bed and Breakfast and the Willard Street Inn.

In the morning, choose between breakfast at the Athens Diner in Colchester, owned by the same husband-and-wife team as Henry's, or the Parkway Diner in South Burlington. Head to the Parkway early to interact with locals and enjoy the banter between the regulars and the workers. At the Parkway, don't miss the Corned Beef Hash or, for lunch, the impressive burgers at extremely fair prices. With so much to do in Burlington, either choose to spend another night in Chittenden County or head for the Northeast Kingdom, specifically the quaint village of Lyndonville. From Burlington, drive east to one of the most scenic and rural areas of the state. The drive is about two hours when you take Route 15 along the way. Stop in Johnson and the Johnson Woolen Mill or in Greensboro to visit the best brewery in the world—as ranked by Rate Beer—Hill Farmstead Brewery. In St. Johnsbury, visit Dog Mountain, an art gallery and dog chapel featuring the work of the late Stephen Huneck. In Greensboro, close to Lyndonville, stay at the Highland Lodge, or make your way to St. Johnsbury for the evening and make the Rabbit Hill Inn or West Hill Bed and Breakfast your home. While in the Northeast Kingdom, go on a tour of the covered bridges in the area, including the Randall Bridge, Chamberlain Mill Bridge, Sanborn Run Bridge, Millers Run Bridge and School House Bridge.

In the morning, head to the Miss Lyndonville Diner and plan to spend some time inside. The essence of the community is embodied in this well-loved local eatery. From Lyndonville, take Route 2 to Montpelier, Vermont's capital, and take in the gold-capped capitol building while walking downtown. Start making your way toward southern Vermont and the Windsor Diner by Interstate 89. In Windsor, visit the Artisan Park and observe glassblowing at the Simon Pearce factory or visit Harpoon Brewing for a tour of the brewery and some samples. Across the parking lot, you'll also find Silo Distillery for samples of a wide range of spirits, including Lavender Vodka. At the Windsor Diner on Main Street in Windsor, the birthplace of Vermont, try a filling classic meal like Liver and Onions or the Fish Fry Dinner on certain days of the week. Not far from Windsor is the Springfield Royal Diner, which is a must-visit for the rarity of the Mahony dining car. Even if solely for an afternoon cup of coffee and a cupcake or slice of pie or a quick stop for coffee in the morning, make a point to visit and admire the subtleties of the space. In this region, consider staying at the Snapdragon Inn or the Weathersfield Inn in Weathersfield, a tiny rural community close to Windsor. Next, make room for a hearty breakfast among locals at the Country Girl Diner in Chester. Save room for the Maple Walnut Pie or try a milkshake from the authentic milkshake maker; who says you can't have dessert with breakfast? In Chester, visit the quaint downtown and the antique stores and art galleries before heading south for an afternoon bite at the Miss Bellows Falls in the town of Rockingham and other sites in the National Register of Historic Places in the industrial town. Note the barrel ceiling and how so little inside has changed while filling up for a late lunch.

Through a road trip to experience Vermont's roadside eateries, it will quickly become apparent how the classic diners of Vermont embody the brand of and the qualities for which the Green Mountain State has become known and prides itself on. When so much in the world changes on a daily basis, so little ever evolves at diners. Diners will continue to bring together neighbors and strangers, unify generations and showcase the essence of Vermont.

Appendix 1
CLASSIC DINER LINGO

In the 1800s, diner slang was used as a form of oral shorthand to quickly communicate orders in a busy setting. Somewhat tongue-in-cheek, this diner language of its own gained widespread usage from the 1920s to the 1970s as a way to communicate efficiently from waitstaff to cook over the loud diner environment, humming with conversation. The colorful phrases and new meanings to common words have become a language in and of itself in diners. Although much of this classic diner slang has died out since the 1970s, many diners in Vermont and beyond celebrate the longevity of their waitstaff, with many employees working for decades in the same diner. Perhaps if you come along a seasoned short-order cook or waitress, you might just hear nuggets of this unique language developed in diners. Even then, Vermont was known for its maple syrup, as indicated by the term "stack of Vermont," referring to pancakes served with maple syrup, and simply "Vermont" as the shorthand for syrup.

Here is a sample selection of quintessential diner jargon to preserve a bit of nostalgia tied to vintage diner vernacular. How many of these phrases do you recognize from modern-day lingo?

5: a glass of milk
21: a glass of limeade
41: a glass of lemonade
50-50: a cup of coffee with half-and-half
51: a cup of hot chocolate

55: a glass of root beer
81: a glass of water
86: remove an item from the menu
Adam's ale: Water
all day: altogether
all hot: baked potato
all the way: served with all the toppings (typically on a burger)
Arnold Palmer: half lemonade and half iced tea
Atlanta: Coca-Cola
axle grease: butter
baby juice: milk
baled hay: Shredded Wheat cereal
balloon juice: soda water
bank: cash register
battery acid: grapefruit juice
beef-on-weck: a type of roast beef sandwich
belch water: seltzer water
belly warmer: coffee
bird: chicken
birdseed: breakfast cereal
birds in a nest: a piece of toast with a hole cut in the middle with a fried egg inside
black and blue: rare meat
blond and sweet/blond with sand: coffee with milk and sugar
bloodhound in the hay: a hot dog with sauerkraut
blowout patches: pancakes
BLT: bacon, lettuce and tomato on toast with mayo
blue plate special: a meal of meat, potatoes and vegetables served on a plate that was typically blue with three sections
board: slice of toast
boiled leaves: tea
bow wow: hot dog
break a cowboy: western omelet
breath: onion
brick: biscuit
bubble dancer: dishwasher
bucket of cold mud: chocolate ice cream
bun pup: hot dog
burn one: put a hamburger on the grill

burn the British: English muffin, toasted
butcher's revenge: meatloaf
cable car: open-faced sandwich
campers: customers who hang out and use a table for an extended period of time
cats' heads and easy diggings: biscuits and gravy
checkerboard: waffle
chicks on a raft: eggs on toast
China: rice pudding
chopper: knife
clean up the kitchen: hash
cluck and grunt: eggs and bacon
coffee dry: coffee with only sugar
coffee high: coffee with only cream
coffee high and dry: coffee with no cream or sugar
cops and robbers: donut and coffee
cow feed: salad
cow juice: milk
cow paste: butter
creep: beer on draught
cup of joe/cup of mud: coffee
deadeye: poached egg
dish pig: dishwasher
dog and maggot: cracker and cheese
dog biscuit: cracker
don't cry over it: no onions
dough well done with cow to cover: toast with butter
drag one through Wisconsin: with cheese on it
drown the kids: boiled eggs
dry: sandwich, burger or hot dog without any condiments
echo: repeat
eggs up: eggs unflipped with unbroken yolks
elephant dandruff: cornflakes
Eve with a lid on: apple pie
firehouse it: add hot sauce to a dish
first lady: spare ribs
fish eyes: tapioca pudding
flop two: two fried eggs, over easy
foreign entanglements: spaghetti

frog sticks: French fries
fry two, let the sun shine: two eggs, sunny side up with unbroken yolks
gallery: booth
Georgia pie: peach pie
give it wings: serve it quickly
go for a walk: to pack something up for take out
grass: lettuce
gravel train: sugar bowl
groundhog: hot dog
hail: ice
heart attack on a rack: biscuits and gravy
hemorrhage: ketchup
hockey puck: hamburger well done
hold the hail: no ice
hot top: hot chocolate
hounds on an island: hot dogs and beans
houseboat: banana split
hug one: orange juice
in the alley: served on the side
in the weeds: when a cook is overworked/overloaded with orders
Irish turkey: corned beef and cabbage
Jewish round: bagel
keep off the grass: hold the lettuce
leg off a pair of trousers: one cup of coffee
let it work: takeout order
life preserver: doughnut
lighthouse: salt shaker
looseners: prunes
love apples: tomatoes
LTO: lettuce, tomato and onion
lumber: toothpick
machine oil: syrup
magoo: custard pie
make it moo: add milk to coffee
mama: marmalade
Mike and Ike: salt and pepper shakers
moo juice: milk
motor oil: syrup
mousetrap: grilled cheese sandwich

Murphy: potato
mystery in the alley: side order of hash
nervous pudding: Jell-O
no cow: without milk
on a rail: fast
on the hoof: meat cooked rare
on wheels: to go
paint it red: put ketchup on it
pair of drawers: two cups of coffee
pigs in a blanket: sausage link wrapped in a pancake
Pittsburgh: something burning
plate of dicks: plate of sausages
Pop Benedict: eggs Benedict
put a hat on it: add ice cream (pie a la mode)
put out the lights and cry: liver and onions
rabbit food: lettuce
radio sandwich: tuna fish sandwich
raft: toast
roller: sausage link
sand: sugar
schmeer: cream cheese on a bagel
sea dust: salt
shake one in the hay: strawberry milkshake
shingle with a shimmy and a shake: toast with butter and jam
shoot from the South: Coca-Cola
smear: butter
soup jockey: waitress
spot with a twist: cup of tea with lemon
stack of Vermont: pancakes with maple syrup
sun kiss: orange juice
sunny-side up: fried eggs, unturned without the yolk broken
sweep the floor: hash
tube steak: hot dog
Vermont: maple syrup
walking: to go
walking in: new order for the kitchen
wart: olive
wax: American cheese
whiskey: rye bread

whiskey down: rye toast
white cow: vanilla milkshake
why bother: decaf coffee with nonfat milk
the works: all condiments on a hamburger, hot dog or sandwich
wrecked and crying: scrambled eggs with onion
wreck 'em: scrambled eggs
yellow blanket on a dead cow: cheeseburger
yellow paint: mustard
zeppelin: sausage

Appendix 2

CLASSIC DINERS OF VERMONT DIRECTORY

Athens Diner
(802) 655-3455
46 Highpoint Center
Colchester, Vermont 05446

Birdseye Diner
(802) 468-5817
590 Main Street
Castleton, Vermont 05735
birdseyediner.com

Blue Benn Diner
(802) 442-5140
314 North Street
Bennington, Vermont 05201

Bob's Diner
(802) 362-4681
2279 Depot Street
Manchester, Vermont 05255
Facebook.com/
bobsdinermanchester

Chelsea Royal Diner
(802) 254-8399
487 Marlboro Road
Brattleboro, Vermont 05301
chelsearoyaldiner.com

Country Girl Diner
(802) 875-1003
46 Vermont Route 103
Chester, Vermont 05143
countrygirldiner.com

The Diner
(802) 388-2397
66 Merchants Row
Middlebury, Vermont 05753
thedinervt.com

Henry's Diner
(802) 862-9010
155 Bank Street
Burlington, Vermont 05401
henrysdinervt.com

Miss Bellows Falls Diner
(802) 463-3700
90 Rockingham Street
Bellows Falls, Vermont 05101

Miss Lyndonville Diner
(802) 626-9890
686 Broad Street
Lyndonville, Vermont 05851

The Parkway Diner
(802) 652-1155
1696 Williston Road
South Burlington, Vermont 05403

The Public House at Quechee Gorge
(802) 295-8500
5813 Woodstock Road, Quechee, Vermont 05059

Springfield Royal Diner
(802) 591-4374
363 River Street (Route 106)
Springfield, Vermont 05156
springfieldroyaldiner.com

The Windsor Diner
(802) 674-5555
135 Main Street
Windsor, Vermont 05089
Facebook.com/1952vt

Appendix 3

DIRECTORY OF VERMONT EATERIES OFFERING A DINER EXPERIENCE

Anthony's Diner
(802) 748-3613
321 Railroad Street
St. Johnsbury, Vermont 05819

Dot's Restaurant
(802) 464-7284
3 West Main Street
Wilmington, Vermont 05363

Erica's American Diner
(802) 849-0205
951 Main Street
Fairfax, Vermont 05454

The Guilty Plate Diner
(802) 399-2011
164 Porters Point Road
Colchester, Vermont 05446

Halfway House Restaurant
(802) 897-5160
450 VT-22A
Shoreham, Vermont 05770

Handy's Lunch
(802) 864-5963
74 Maple Street
Burlington, Vermont 05401

Hartland Diner
(802) 436-3663
159 US-5
Hartland, Vermont 05048

Laura B's
(802) 893-4400
3 Southerberry Drive
Milton, Vermont 05468

Maple City Diner
(802) 528-8400
17 Swanton Road
St Albans City, Vermont 05478

The Maple Diner
(802) 396-0045
US-4
Bridgewater, Vermont 05035

Martha's Diner
(802) 754-6800
585 T-5
Coventry, Vermont 05825

Maxi's Restaurant
(802) 244-0910
47 North Main Street
Waterbury, Vermont 05676

The Milton Diner
(802) 893-1743
514 US-7
Milton, Vermont 05468

P&H Truck Stop
(802) 429-2141
2886 US-302
Wells River, Vermont 05081

Papa Pete's
(802) 681-0181
1104 Woodford Road
Bennington, Vermont 05201

The Public House at Quechee Gorge
(802) 295-8500
5813 Woodstock Road
Quechee, Vermont 05059

Rosie's Restaurant
(802) 388-7052
886 US-7
Middlebury, Vermont 05753

St. Albans Diner
(802) 528-8505
8 Swanton Road
St Albans City, Vermont 05478

The Sugar and Spice Vermont Sugar House
(802) 773-7832
45 US-4
Mendon, Vermont 05701

Sunny Side Diner
(802) 442-9900
241 VT-9
Bennington, Vermont 05201

Tot's Diner
(802) 287-2213
25 Main Street
Poultney, Vermont 05764

The Townshend Dam Diner
(802) 874-4107
5353 VT-30
Townshend, Vermont 05353

ABOUT THE AUTHOR

Erin McCormick is a Vermont enthusiast who travels the state to discover the best of the best in Vermont—all from a local's perspective. She runs the popular blog Travel Like a Local: Vermont, where she highlights restaurants, inns, breweries, boutiques, hikes, swimming holes, scenic views and, now, Vermont's best classic eateries to showcase the special place that is Vermont.

When she's not road tripping (or eating her way) across the Green Mountain State, Erin is a Vermont Realtor and a marketer for Vermont businesses. Erin lives in Colchester, Vermont, with her partner, Nick, and two rescue dogs, Sally and Buford.